DEAR KATIE

KATIE BOYLE

TVTimes
FAMILY BOOKS

INDEPENDENT TELEVISION BOOKS LTD, LONDON

INDEPENDENT TELEVISION BOOKS LTD, LONDON

247 Tottenham Court Road
London W1P 0AU

© Katie Boyle 1975

ISBN 0 900 72736 5

Printed in Great Britain by
Butler & Tanner Ltd
Frome and London

Also available in this series:

BEATING THE COST OF COOKING
Mary Berry
CARAVANNING
Barry Williams
HOUSE PLANTS MADE EASY
Jean Taylor
KNOW YOUR CAR
John Dyson
KNOW YOUR RIGHTS
Dr Michael Winstanley and
Ruth Dunkley
POWER TOOLS AT HOME
Harold King

ACKNOWLEDGEMENTS
The author thanks all those readers who have contributed to this collection of tips and also William Timyn for the dog illustrations, and Mary French and Francine Block for the other drawings.

CONTENTS

Introduction

An introduction to a book is supposed to give some idea of what it's about. Well, in this case, it's not awfully easy (have a look at the contents). So, instead of 'what', I'll tell you 'why' I've written it.

When the 'Dear Katie' page first started I said I'd do my best to reply to any queries readers of the *TVTimes* cared to drop me a line about. I wasn't setting up either as a 'know-all', imparting abstract wisdom, or an agony-soothing Aunt Sal, but I have stumbled on quite a few facts of life (one tends to when one's been around for a while) and have muddled through my own medley of mistakes. What's more I've been lucky enough to meet experts in lots of fields (fashion, beauty, health, housekeeping etc etc). This, combined with my built-in mania for asking questions and absorbing sponge-like the answers, made me feel that I might be able to help others. I remember adding that maybe we could swop information sometimes and make it a two way pen-pals act.

Well that was way back, and your response surpassed my highest hopes! Together we've touched on all kinds of subjects—from tips on how to pack, to preparing pasta! From how to pluck eyebrows (painlessly, of course) to patching up pimples—not to mention the attempts on occasions to mend broken hearts. And among my mountainous weekly mail comes a steady flow of letters complaining that a copy of our page, with a particular tip on it, has been mislaid, and suggesting I could make things easier for everyone by putting all the information into a book.

That, quite simply, is how this book began.

Somehow, though, rather like Topsy in *Uncle Tom's Cabin*, it . . . 'growed', and you'll find lots of extra bits and pieces that have never been in the *TVTimes*. I just hope some of them will be of interest to every one of you, because they all interest me.

As far as the actual tips go, I promise they're the kind that really work, not, like others I know, which just make the initial problems worse. But I realise that as soon as I've sent this manuscript off to the printers, I'll kick myself for not including the one about . . . and that one . . . and of course that super other one . . .! I'm quite sure that you too will have more to add, so I've left a few blank pages at the back where you can scribble them down.

I do hope all the same that this 'non-comprehensive' hotch potch of information will help to smooth out some of the wrinkles of everyday living, and possibly give you a few laughs into the bargain.

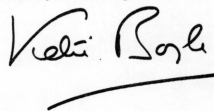

Household

Buying sense

READ INSTRUCTIONS OF EVERY AND ANYTHING YOU BUY. A lot of time and thought has been spent on writing them ... TO HELP THE CONSUMER. So if you chuck them out with the wrapping you're doing a disservice to yourself, the goods and the manufacturer, and it COULD sometimes be dangerous.

The chemist's   You can cut down your chemist's bills by asking for the 'BP equivalent' of your favourite brand remedies. BP means British Pharmacopoeia, the official list of permitted drugs and usages. You'll pay much less for their version, the formula is probably the same.

Duty free shops at airports may be abolished within the next few years, but until they are, do some window-shopping here in Britain before you go abroad: then you'll know exactly what you are saving on which items — if anything, at times. Bring back price lists from duty free shops and plan for the next time.

Linen   Watch out for cheap sheets and pillow-cases which have a lot of dressing to disguise their poor quality. They'll go all limp and thin when washed. Rub two parts of the same sheet together — if lots of white 'powder' falls out, don't buy, there's more dressing than quality there.

Cornered hems are stronger than hem-stitched ones.

When buying pillow-cases, make sure they're two to three inches wider and eight inches longer than the pillows — then they'll fit without straining at the seams.

When you buy sheets make allowances for a generous tucking-in at both sides and at the foot of the bed. Beds and bedding have gone metric now, and the Metrication Board gives the following measurements:

	Bed size	Blanket size	Blended sheets*	Cotton and flannelette sheets*
Small single (corresponding to the old 3 ft × 6 ft 3 in bed)	90 cm × 190 cm	180 cm × 240 cm	175 cm × 260 cm	175 cm × 255 cm 175 cm × 275 cm 200 cm × 255 cm 200 cm × 275 cm
Standard single	100 cm × 200 cm	200 cm × 250 cm	175 cm × 260 cm	175 cm × 275 cm 200 cm × 275 cm
Small double (corresponding to the old 4 ft 6 in × 6 ft 3 in bed)	135 cm × 190 cm	230 cm × 250 cm	230 cm × 260 cm	230 cm × 255 cm 230 cm × 275 cm
Standard double	150 cm × 200 cm	260 cm × 250 cm	230 cm × 260 cm	230 cm × 275 cm
Extra large	300 cm × 280 cm		275 cm × 275 cm	270 cm × 295 cm

All these sizes provide for an adequate 'tuck-in' allowance.

*Sheets are now increasingly made from blends of man-made fibre and cotton; they usually offer less shrinkage than the traditional cotton and flannelette sheets, and either less or no ironing.

Mattresses vary widely in thickness, and this affects the size of the flat sheets for a particular bed and the amount of tuck-in provided.

Fitted sheets are made to fit particular lengths and widths of mattresses, and are labelled according to mattress size. They are normally designed for a mattress of average thickness (18 cm to 20 cm or 7 in to 8 in).

Continental duvets certainly take a lot of toil out of bed making but buy them with at least a generous foot and a half or more overlay all round the bed or they'll defeat their purpose and slip off or climb up and give you cold feet.

Don't be rule-bound — if you feel extra chilly a duvet will still lie snugly over an easy to wash courtelle (or similar) blanket.

General household hints

I've gathered together lots of tips covering so many different subjects that I've had to collect them under one 'General' heading. Some of them are money-saving ideas – watch for the '£' sign in the margin.

£ **Batteries**   Wrap an apparently dead battery in tinfoil and place it in the oven when you're cooking – it'll come to life again. A small battery should stay in a moderately hot oven for 20 minutes, larger sized ones recharge with the same moderate heat if left for 30 minutes.

Blankets (clean woollen) can be stored in large bin-liners – but put a few sheets of newspaper in with them and seal tightly to ensure they're moth-proof.

Candles   To snuff out candles without spraying wax over the table, hold your finger between yourself and the wick, near to the wick, and blow across it.

If candles are too small for the holders, just hold a lighted match underneath the candle and, when the wax is soft, press it down.

Candles have lots of uses apart from decorative ones – run one up and down a stiff zip, for example, or on stiff sash cords or a drawer that sticks, and these problems will smooth out. Or roll one over your writing on an envelope and it won't smudge in the rain.

Chamois leather   A small piece will do bigger jobs if you sew it into the middle of a large soft duster – you'll then only be crumpling the duster and every inch of the chamois will be working.

Child artists   Children will have no excuse to write on the walls if you cut off the top and bottom of washing-up liquid bottles, wash and dry them. Then flatten them overnight under a few heavy books. In the morning you'll have some washable scribbling pads. With felt pens and a small damp sponge to wipe them clean, children can use these over and over again.

Incidentally, Dad's old shirts make splendid and practical painting smocks and overalls for small children. Cut off the cuffs, put narrow hems round the sleeves and thread elastic through. Level the hem of the shirt and put it on the child back to front.

China and glass   To store for any length of time or to pack for posting. Squirt a little washing-up liquid into a bowl of warm water and dip a sheet of newspaper into it, wet it thoroughly then press it dry and wrap tidily around each article. Stand them where they can dry safely and the newspaper will harden into a protective coating. You can then pack each object into a sturdy box with no fears. If posting, add some slim foam rubber for extra protection. I don't suggest you try, but I dropped two glasses so wrapped onto a stone floor once and when I opened my eyes they were still whole!

Cold in bed?   To keep warm in bed in an icy room, spread layers of newspaper between two or more blankets – used dry cleaning plastic covers will protect the blankets from the newsprint.

Decanters   To get out a glass stopper stuck in a decanter, warm a little oil (preferably vegetable oil) and let it seep down the sides of the stopper. Leave the decanter overnight in a really warm place – not in a direct heat however – and the stopper should coax loose in the morning. If not, another dose of warm oil over the next 24 hours should do the trick.

Door-stop   Make a bag about 10 in × 2 in out of a strong piece of furnishing fabric. Fill it with old nylons and attach a loop at each end. Hitch one loop over the handle on one side of the door and the second loop on the handle the other side. Now the door can swing to and fro without banging or catching fingers.

Fire kindling   If you're lucky enough to have an open fire, it still needs kindling. Keep all empty waxed containers (ice-cream and milk cartons, etc) and all candle stubs – these will set things alight with no effort at all.

Glass   See **China and glass** above.

Hot water bottles If yours leaks, there's still a use for it. Cut off the top and bottom, slit open one side and glue it to a wooden step to make it non-slippery.

£ Lining drawers, shelves etc When using a sticky-backed paper, only take off a small triangle under the four corners. It'll stick down just as well, and you can easily take it up and use again somewhere else another time.

Loo freshness Always keep a box of matches in the loo — but never with children around — strike a couple after paying a visit and there'll be no unpleasant trace left behind.

Medicines To prevent accidents, weed out that medicine chest every so often. Chemicals can deteriorate with age, so flush down the loo the contents of all bottles and those with faded labels or none at all. Crush pills and pull the chain on them too.

Do label all bottles, especially dangerous medicines or poisons like paraquat, and don't store them in squash bottles which children might get hold of.

Incidentally, if you've got to take a filthy-tasting medicine, you'll forget it quickly if you suck an ice-cube before and afterwards — it'll freeze the taste buds.

Mothballs If you believe in mothballs and lots of them to protect woollen blankets and clothes, you can get rid of their smell when you want to. Just sprinkle powdered charcoal onto paper and leave it in drawers or on shelves. Powdered charcoal sewn into little muslin bags, then put into pockets, will kill the smell of mothballs in furs or other clothes.

Ornaments Little squares of felt or baize stuck onto the bottom of ornaments, ashtrays, etc will stop the furniture getting scratched. Don't get them wet when cleaning the ornaments — felt isn't washable — and if they're put back damp they'll leave a watermark.

Parcels When doing up a parcel, dip the string into water and wring it out before tying it — this way it'll shrink as it dries and grip more firmly.

If you're using *nylon* cord or rope, seal the ends so that they don't fray. Light a match and hold it to the 'raw' ends — the fibres will 'melt' together. Don't use this on cotton rope or string though!

Pictures To prevent pictures from leaving a mark against the wall, stick small squares of felt or baize at the back on the bottom two corners (this trick also stops cigarette boxes and heavy ornaments from scratching furniture tops).

Pillows If there's a left-over smell of bird in a feather-filled pillow, this old-fashioned cleaning method should get rid of it. Fill the bath full of warm water, add a few handfuls of soap-flakes and whip up to a lather. Put two pillows in this mixture and walk up and down on them in the bath, treading the suds right through (yes, just as they treat grapes in wine-making). If the water comes out scummy, run it out and start all over again. Rinse several times, then dry the pillows out of doors, in the sunshine if possible, and shake frequently.

Plastic egg boxes (the less flimsy kind) will take a coat or more of paint and make out-of-the-ordinary if not everlasting holders for tin tacks, paper clips, stamps etc.

Plastic trays with divisions are best lined with baize or foam rubber to keep cutlery unscratched.

Rubber gloves If your right-hand glove always splits first, keep the left £ one. Then, when the same thing happens with another pair, just turn the odd left-over one inside out, and you'll have a pair again. Or mend a small split by sticking a strip of waterproof plaster on the outside *and* inside of the glove.

Runners A touch of Vaseline or cooking oil will ease reluctant runners on curtains and doors, and will stop most household joints squeaking.

£ **Soap** Left-over bits of soap are useful and fun for the children's bath-time if sewn between two bits of foam rubber cut into animal or fish shapes, or just plain squares.

£ Here's another way of using scraps of soap. Shred them, put them in an empty margarine container and cover them with boiling water. Stir well, then let the mixture dry out and you'll have a tablet of soap.

£ Bath soap and candles will last longer when you come to use them if they're stored in a warm place like your linen or airing cupboard. Nicely scented soap will make your linen smell good too.

£ **Toothpaste** When you think your toothpaste is finished, press any remains down towards the tail, then snip off the tube. You will probably find a few more days' supply inside.

Towels Always wash new terry towels before using them, because in the manufacturing process loose-spun yarns are looped into the foundation fabric – it's these that make the towels absorbent – but the loops are easy to pull out in the wash or in use when they're soft and new. When they've been washed a few times the groundwork will tighten and hold the loops firmly. Any left-over long strands can be safely snipped off with a pair of sharp scissors without hurting the towel.

£ Good parts of old towels cut down and hemmed make good flannels.

Typing noise If you're burning the midnight oil typing, put a bath towel or blanket under the machine and the neighbours are less likely to complain.

Untidy? If you're untidy by nature, it does help to have a dumping drawer for things and a large dumping folder for letters, bills, receipts etc. At least you'll know that 'it's in there – somewhere'!

£ **Wrapping paper** Don't throw away used fancy wrapping paper. Level off any torn edges, then press it with a warm iron. You'll save quite a few pennies at Christmas and birthday times.

Do-it-yourself tips

A bedhead without much character can be covered with the same material you use for the curtains. But if you can't afford a bedspread in the same pattern, get or dye one in the background shade of the curtains.

Draught stopper To make one of those 'sausages' to keep out draughts under doors, fill stockings of the leg part of tights with sawdust, cover the sausage with plastic/cling film, then sew them up and cover them with any material or colour which will blend with your decor.

Looking glass An unframed looking glass can take on more character if edged with a strip of the curtain material 2 in wide. Either stick the fabric straight onto the glass or pad it with foam rubber for a 'raised' effect. Sticky dressmaking or office tape rolled or folded so as to take in the glass and the material holds it in place.

Nails If you're going to drive a nail into a plaster wall, put a bit of sticky tape on the wall first and pierce through it – the plaster shouldn't crack with this method.

Rawlplugs It's easier to put a rawlplug into a hollow wall if you bend a hairpin into a 'U with wings'. Put this into the wall first, then shove in the rawlplug.

Tiles Drilling through tiles tends to be . . . 'slippery'. So put sticky tape over the spot - you can take it off afterwards.

Tools will never go rusty in a toolbox if you add a few pieces of balls of camphor.

Carpet care

Cleaning

Don't use a vacuum cleaner on a newly laid carpet as it will suction out a lot of the lasting quality and clog the cleaner at the same time. The pile needs to settle and be down-trodden for several weeks. To clean up during this time, use a carpet sweeper very lightly.

When you start using a vacuum cleaner after the initial 'resting' period, still watch that it doesn't clog up. Change the bags often and give the air an extra chance to run through the cleaner while you're doing a room by tipping it up from the carpet whilst keeping it running.

Carpets can be kept beautifully when the vacuum cleaner is inadvisable and *always* round the skirting boards where a sweeper or vacuum cleaner will never reach, by wiping over with a sponge cloth wrung out in carpet shampoo (diluted according to the instructions). Take a dish-washing bowl of shampoo per room, then dip and wring out a sponge cloth, wiping the carpet as you go.

To deal with specific stains on carpets, have a look under the *Stain removing* section on pages 13–16 where I deal with individual stains such as ink, wine, puppy-puddles and cigarette burns.

Rugs

Thick foam-rubber strips stuck to the underneath of rugs will help to stop them slipping. The only permanent remedy is to sew them onto fitted carpets – but have this done professionally.

Car sense

Paint protection To avoid the paintwork being chipped off car doors when opened in the garage, stuff old tights inside each other to form bolsters – then dangle strategically down the garage wall. A few more 'danglers' could be useful on the end of the wall if you tend to misjudge the length of the car. As an alternative, and if you can find any, attach a sheet of thick foam rubber to the sides and end walls of the garage.

A sheet of foam rubber looped to the wing mirrors and back bumpers will protect the sides of your car if it lodges in a multi-car park.

Petrol caps In case your petrol cap is stolen from the car or you drive off without it after a fill-up, keep a jampot cap (the twist-on kind) in your car as a 'spare'. Make sure it's the right size for your tank!

Plan ahead when driving, don't make the car in front your horizon.

Relaxed driving Curl your thumbs loosely round the steering wheel when driving, it'll relax you. Resting your thumbs along the wheel stiffens your arms from wrists right to the back of the neck nerves, which is tiring in the long run.

Spare keys Don't only keep a spare set of car keys at home but write down the number of each key in your pocket diary.

Windscreens should not freeze up on icy mornings if there are two or three dessertspoonsful of methylated spirit in the car's water-spraying container.

To prevent windscreens fugging-up on a cold day, just wipe a slice of raw potato over the glass inside before setting off.

Cleaning and polishing

Hardware stores try to keep up with all the latest cleaning products for every kind of surface – so if in doubt about the bath, some rust on chrome, or whatever, go browse around or ask the manager's advice if an assistant hasn't got the answer.

Below, I've listed lots of hints on how to clean and polish individual items, from aluminium pans to windows. For dealing with specific stains, see the *Stain removing* section on pages 13–16.

Aluminium pans   To clean a badly stained aluminium pan, simply stew some rhubarb in it and the grey and black marks will vanish.

Brass   When cleaning those awkwardly shaped brass fittings, cut the shape of the key-hole, handle or whatever it is out of a piece of cardboard. Slip it over the fitting and you won't leave polish marks on the door or furniture.

Even very or anciently dirty brass will shine again if rubbed with some Duraglit wadding moistened with ordinary household ammonia. If you want a less 'brassy' look, use the silver Duraglit.

If you want to lacquer your brass, clean and polish it brightly, then put newspaper on the floor in a warm, dust-free room and spray or brush the lacquer onto the brass. Hardware and do-it-yourself shops stock lacquer.

To strip lacquer off brass, wipe the surface clean with a damp cloth, dry it, then apply a paint stripper with a fine brush. In a minute or so when the lacquer bubbles, rinse it off with plenty of cold water. If the lacquer's been on quite a while, you'll probably have to repeat the process from start to finish once or twice.

Cards   Wipe plastic cards with a damp cloth; paper cards will come up well with cotton wool moistened with spirits of camphor or methylated spirit, and a final stroke over with a clean cloth.

Chamois leather   Chamois leather *can* be washed at home *and* kept soft and supple. Wash it in warm, soapy suds, pressing and squeezing as with wool. Rinse three times in warm water, adding a drop of vinegar to the final rinse. Squeeze out surplus water...then *smear* pure olive oil on the chamois, working it in gently. Finally dry away from direct heat and preferably out of doors.

An alternative way of keeping it soft is to leave some of the soap in— after getting all the dirt out.

China   Tea and coffee stains can be taken off china using dry denture powder, or bicarbonate of soda, or a solution of damp salt. Rub gently round the surface with a tissue or paper cloth—this method won't damage even the most delicate enamelling. Rinse china well before re-use.

For very precious china, the Victoria and Albert Museum uses warm water only, never using detergents which might make the china slippery and increase the risk of breakage. A *small* amount of bleach is sometimes added, but all detergents of any kind must be kept away from gilding.

Furniture   Polished furniture which is really cared for does need a once or twice a year wash down to get rid of the inevitable build-up of polish and, despite regular dusting, the accumulated dirt. Here are two 'refreshers'.

1 Two teaspoonsful of malt vinegar to one breakfast cup of warm water. Apply with a soft clean cloth dipped in the liquid and wrung out. Wipe over the surface a number of times. Wipe completely dry and leave the furniture to breathe for an hour or so before putting on a new and light film of polish.
2 To one quart of hot water add 3 tablespoonsful of raw or boiled linseed oil, and 2 tablespoonsful of gum turpentine. Mix well and let it cool. With a soft cloth dipped and wrung out in this concoction 'wash' a small area at a time and dry it as you go along. Repolish afterwards and once again use only a light film of polish.

In the long run there's no substitute for a little polish and a lot of elbow grease. The alternative is a tacky, dust-catching surface. A good guide is to run a clean finger on the part you've just polished—it should leave no mark at all on the finish.

If you should want to make your own furniture polish (though I can't think why) buy a quart of boiled linseed oil and a pint of turpentine and mix these well together. Then keep in a jar or tin with lid on—use sparingly.

When polishing, always rub in the same direction as the wood grain.

Always dust with clean, dry and HEMMED dusters—unhemmed ones leave fluff and can even damage the finish.

Friars Balsam left on for a few hours will help camouflage white stains on dark woods. Polish as usual over the Friars Balsam.

White and other marks will disappear from woodwork if treated with a mixture of olive oil and cigarette or cigar ash. Work it well into the furniture and leave on for an hour or so. If the stain is a very old friend, you may have to repeat the process a few times.

A few drops of methylated spirits or brass cleaner on a clean rag rubbed round lightly takes away watermarks from woodwork. Repolish the surface after using this.

Watermarks can also be dealt with by putting several pieces of clean white blotting paper over the ring, pressing with a warm — not *hot* — iron, then rubbing with a little furniture wax applied with steel wool.

Leather furniture needs an extra nourishing session once or twice a year. Oils darken leather, so for the darker shades use a good brand name conditioner. While on light skins, white vaseline or a white cream is better.

If you have the patience, massage the conditioner in with your hands and finger tips, although a clean cloth will do. Then make sure to wipe off thoroughly every trace of grease or you'll get telltale marks on your clothes.

Don't wax leather furniture.

Don't use paraffin on leather — mineral oils aren't good for it.

Hide food is an excellent leather nourisher, but it sinks right in and the finish will be dull and not glossy.

Mock leather   Methylated spirit will take ballpoint pen marks out of mock leather.

Painted furniture should be waxed then it can be washed down every so often. Add a tablespoonful of borax to a quart of soapsudsy water, and another tablespoonful of borax to the rinsing water and it'll be an easy job.

Natural bamboo, reed, cane and wicker furniture should be wiped over regularly with a damp cloth — but to prevent it drying out, becoming brittle and splitting, it should be wet thoroughly once a year, particularly if used in a centrally-heated home. Either put it in the garden and let the garden hose spray it, drinking in the bath, or leave it under the bathroom shower until well dampened. If it's very dirty, wash it with pure soapsuds laced with a dash of ammonia. Dry thoroughly, and give it a coat of shellac. If painted and if the paint can take water, give it the same annual treatment, although it won't be quite so rejuvenating.

Furs — fun and others — particularly useful for light-coloured collars and cuffs, as well as fur rugs. Heat some bran or oatmeal in a bowl in the oven. When hot, sprinkle generously onto the fur and work in with fingers. Leave it on for a while to act as a dry shampoo, then shake out thoroughly and if possible hang in the open air. Then comb through with care.

Glass decanter   To clean a stained glass decanter, cut some newspaper into small squares and drop inside, add a little water, swill around, then leave overnight. Next morning swoosh out the paper — a final spin of hot detergent will complete this re-sparkling process.

Another decanter cleaner: put two teaspoonsful of denture powder into the decanter and fill it up with warm water. Leave it to stand for a few minutes, then rinse out.

And another: leave neat vinegar in decanter overnight. Rinse out with warm water next morning.

...and one more: you'll find that the lead shot out of a cartridge no. 9 laced with cold water also does the trick!

Iron   To clean an iron, wrap a white candle stub in a clean bit of linen and rub over the hot iron surface. Then rub the cleaned iron over another scrap of linen to finish the job.

Jewellery   According to a number of jewellers, precious stones set in silver, gold or platinum will sparkle more than usual if rubbed with a soft toothbrush in warm water laced with washing-up liquid. This will not loosen the setting of real — repeat *real* — jewellery.

To clean 'soft stones' such as turquoises, opals and the like, swish round in an egg-cupful of gin.

Water and mild detergents are fine for the hard stones, such as diamonds, sapphires, rubies, emeralds.

Kettle   Brand products are sold in hardware shops to de-fur kettles, but to do it yourself, put a level dessertspoonful of borax into a kettle full of cold water and bring it to the boil. Empty the kettle and rinse thoroughly before using. You may have to repeat this procedure once or twice if it has furred up badly, and wipe out any remaining residue with a stick-mop.

Another method is to put a few tablespoonsful of water softener into a kettle filled with cold water and bring it to the boil. This time leave it to get cold before rinsing out well. Repeat if necessary.

Yet another kettle defurrer is denture powder! Quarter fill the kettle and when the water boils, put a heaped teaspoonful of denture powder in it – don't worry, it will fizz up like crazy but won't explode! Leave it to cool off, then empty and fill up with clean water again.

Plastic   White plastic sieves that have become discoloured can easily be brought back to new by leaving overnight in a solution of water and household bleach. Rinse well the next day.

Silver   Keep silver cutlery clean by wrapping it in green baize. The atmosphere will not get at it and it won't need cleaning so often.

To get rid of those black egg stains on silver spoons: put three silver milk-bottle tops and 2 tablespoons of household soda into a pint of boiling water. Dip the spoons in the mixture for a couple of minutes to remove the stain – an old toothbrush helps.

Sponges   Cellulose sponges will clean up if soaked for a few minutes in a mild solution of household bleach. Rinse them carefully, then hang up to dry – but never in the sun or by a radiator or they'll become hard and brittle.

Natural sponges, which are the skeletons of millions of tiny sea animals dried and bleached, can be cleaned by soaking in water and ammonia – 1 tablespoon of ammonia to a quart of water. Rinse well, squeeze out every scrap of water and dry in the shade.

Alternatively, soak your natural sponge for 24 hours in a solution of 1 tablespoon vinegar to 1 pint water. Then rinse in clean water.

Natural sponges will keep well if you hang them up by a loop of string. Never dry them in the sun or on a radiator as they'll become hard and brittle.

Telephone   Use a very tightly wrung-out damp cloth in Listerine-laced water to clean the phone. The PO say it's not necessary to disinfect the mouthpiece as a rule, but when needed use methylated spirits on a pad of cotton wool.

Thermos   Hot water with washing-up liquid or hot water with a generous pinch of baking powder will keep a thermos clean. If there's something stuck to the sides, throw in small bits of clean paper. With the liquid, these will act as a mild abrasive. Rinse out thoroughly and stand the flask upside down to drip and dry out. Once dry, leave it uncapped until used again – it'll stay fresher.

Windows   I've found the most successful way of cleaning windows is to use a bucketful of water with a little paraffin poured onto the surface. Don't smoke while you're doing the job! Get hold of a window cleaner's scrim if you can, otherwise a floor cloth will do, and, when you've finished, just rinse it out in clean water – don't wash it in detergents or soap suds.

Here's another method: crumple newspaper, dip it into a bucketful of water, wring out, pat into a pad and wash the panes. Leave the glass to dry and wipe over with a chamois leather.

Stain removing

Speed is the by-word with stain removing – the quicker you are after an accident the more likely you are to get any mark out. But if the material isn't a delicate one, don't be put off trying if the stain's been around quite a while – it just might still fade or even disappear completely.

If the material is delicate, however, or if you're in any doubt whatsoever, take it along to the dry cleaner's and tell them what's the cause of the stain. And if you've already had a go at getting it out, admit it!

N.B. It's wiser to stick to dry cleaners who are members of the Association of British Launderers and Cleaners (just ask the manager for this information (details in list of Associations) because in case of disagreements you have a 'referee').

Basic rules for stain removing

Always try out a solvent on a hidden part of the fabric first, at the hems or seams, to see if the colour runs or the fabric is affected in any way.

Always use cotton wool or blotting paper as a pad underneath the stained material and dab with solvent on top of the stain. Be careful though, and keep renewing pads, because certain things like ink, lipstick, and ballpoint marks go through the fabric onto the pad.

Always work from the outer edge of the stain inwards when using stain removers, so as not to make a ring.

Always 'pinch' stains caused by liquids out of a material – rubbing them in will only cause them to sink further into the fabric.

It often helps to wash out the last traces of the stain with detergent suds while the material is still damp with solvent, working the stain around between your fingers.

Never use water to remove a stain on dyed wild silk or on a moiré pattern which shows only on one side of the fabric.

Basic stain removers

Keep these in the home, clearly labelled, in a cool place, and *out of the children's reach*.

carbon tetrachloride	There are rather more expensive proprietary grease solvents available. Use only by open window if possible – don't breathe in the fumes.
glycerine	
household ammonia	Careful of eyes, skin and don't breathe in the fumes.
hydrogen peroxide	
methylated spirits	
salts of lemon	Rust marks.
turpentine	

When and how to use these removers is given under the list of treatments of individual stains which follows.

Treating individual stains

Alcohol   For a brand-new mark left by wine, run lots of cold water through the mark, followed by washing in detergent suds. But if the fabric is boilable, put it in cold suds, bring them to the boil and keep simmering for ten minutes.

If red wine, liqueur or port is spilt on a carpet, stop it staining by rubbing it over immediately with chunks of ice.

Alcohol, beer and wine also come out of carpets with a teaspoonful of a mixture of borax in half a pint of warm water. Leave a few minutes, then rinse.

Ballpoint pen   Neat methylated spirit, and quite a lot of it, takes most of these marks out of nylon and other man-made fibres, if applied at once. (I've just proved this once again after I tipped my bag out onto my white Marks and Sparks bedspread and the tops came off my red and green pens . . . !)

Meths gets ballpoint pen marks off carpets, woodwork, vinyl, etc. If nothing else has taken it out, always try meths on any hard surface.

Beetroot   A brand-new mark should go after a soak in cold water followed by a wash in detergent suds. But if the fabric is boilable, put it in cold suds, bring to the boil and keep simmering for ten minutes.

On carpets, mop and blot the stains with carpet shampoo until stain has been removed and then rinse off with lukewarm water.

Bicycle oil   See entry under **Nicotine**.

Blood   Never put a new stain into hot water, which will set it. Soak the article in cold, salted water and then wash in detergent suds. If there's still a trace, soak in a solution of hydrogen peroxide for half an hour or so (one part peroxide to nine of water). Rinse well, and wash again.

I've got blood stains off jersey and satin by winding white cotton round my finger, spitting on it, then rubbing it over the material. Be generous with the spittle, but careful not to add any lipstick, and you might need more than one length of cotton.

If the stain is an old one, soak it for a few minutes in cold water with a few drops of ammonia added. Then sponge through with clean cold water to get rid of the smell of ammonia.

Brown stains on a bath   Where the enamel isn't chipping, try a generous application of hydrogen peroxide and cream of tartar mixed to a paste. Leave on overnight. Then rinse off with lashings of cold water next morning. (Hardware stores are always helpful in suggesting effective brand name remedies for this too.)

Candle wax can be taken out of carpets and materials by laying the dull side of thick brown wrapping paper on the wax and ironing over it with a hot iron.

Candle wax comes off polished wood with a touch of lighter fuel on a clean soft duster.

Cigarette burns will come off all washable materials with a piece of ice and a scrape — this method works on carpets too. If there's a stain left over, soak it with cleaning fluid.

Cigarette scorch marks will come off a carpet, if the fibres haven't been damaged, with a rub-over with dry steel wool.

Chewing gum will come off all washable materials and off carpets if rubbed first with ice cubes, then carefully scraped off with a knife. Carbon tetrachloride will get rid of any left over stain. If there is just a sugar stain, sponge it off with water.

Coffee   Small stains on washable material should come out by pouring warm water and liquid detergent repeatedly through the fabric. If the stain's large, have it laundered. If the material isn't washable, take it to the dry cleaner's at once.

Coffee comes off carpets if you lather an egg yolk and a little warm water with a few drops of alcohol. Then rinse with clean water.

Cooking fat   Use carbon tetrachloride with a pad underneath, then wash well with detergent suds. (But don't use carbon tetrachloride on delicate fabrics, and always use it near an open window.)

Dog puddles   A puppy puddle won't stain even the most delicately coloured carpet if you catch it while it's damp. Blot, and pour methylated spirit over it, then rub with a clean cloth, add a bit more meths and leave to dry. This trick works on adult dog puddles and even a male dog's spray on any fabric. Although it's best to deal with this at once I have found meths removes the stain even after it has already dried on, but be generous with it.

An equally effective alternative method which just takes longer to dry is to blot the blunder and squirt soda water over it. Then leave it without mopping or rubbing.

Eggs   Cold water, and lots of it, at once. Or if you've noticed it too late, brush in cold detergent suds with a nail brush before washing. Whatever you do, don't use hot water for egg stains because the albumen in the egg will cook into the fabric.

To remove those black egg stains on spoons, see under **Silver** in the **Cleaning and polishing** section, page 12.

Fruit juices   Attack fruit juices at once—stretch the marked surface over a bowl and keep pouring through warm water laced with detergent.

Grass   Methylated spirit has worked with me, but if it doesn't come out with the first gentle rub, invest in a dry clean.

Hair tint dye   If you had to dilute the tint with peroxide before using and splashed it over a white carpet, a generous drop of peroxide on a pad of cotton wool will rub it out if tackled at once.

Ink   Freshly spilled ink, except for indelible, usually comes out of a carpet if you soak the stains with cold milk, leave the milk on for a few minutes, then blot with blotting paper. You may have to repeat this a few times before washing the carpet with carpet shampoo according to directions. (An old African custom is to mash tomatoes to a pulp and leave on a carpet overnight to clean off all stains—but I haven't had the courage to try this one yet.)

Lemon juice takes ink out of fabrics—but if it has only just been spilt, a soak in cold water will probably get it out.

By the way, most ink stains will come off your fingers if you spit on your finger first, then rub it with the head of a burnt match—but you'll have to wash your hands afterwards as well.

Iron rust is practically impossible to get out of materials which have to be dry cleaned, but on cottons, linens and other washable materials, lemon juice does the trick. Dampen the stain with water, squeeze the juice of a lemon onto it, then hold it in the steam of a boiling kettle for a few minutes. Rinse out with water and do it all over again until the mark has gone.

Another method which works is to sprinkle salt straight onto the stain, add the juice of a lemon but do *not* leave it to dry in the sunshine. Rinse out in cool water. Sunshine can *produce* iron-rust-looking stains if man-made fibres are dried in it.

For getting iron rust stains out of white fabrics, salts of lemon are good. Stretch the stained part of the fabric over a bowl, and put salts of lemon directly onto the rust mark. Pour boiling water through them. Rub with the handle of a wooden spoon—the salts are poisonous. Repeat as often as necessary. This is an excellent remover, but must only be used on *white* fabrics.

Lacquer (hair) comes off woodwork, glass, and patent leather with methylated spirit on a pad of cotton wool.

Lipstick   Use carbon tetrachloride with a pad underneath, then wash well with detergent suds. Test the carbon tetrachloride on the fabric first, however.

Methylated spirit on a pad of cotton wool will usually remove lipstick marks from woodwork, mock leather or plastic.

Make-up comes off clothes (especially synthetic fabrics) with methylated spirit or a little paintbrush restorer on a pad of cotton wool.

Milk   Small stains on washable material should come out by pouring warm water and liquid detergent repeatedly through the fabric. Have large stains laundered. If the material isn't washable, take it to the dry cleaner's at once. Carpet shampoo mixed in warm water gets it out of carpets.

Mildew will come out of a carpet if wiped over with a 50/50 mixture of water and ammonia and left to dry.

Nail varnish   Dab with acetone or nail varnish remover, except on rayons and acetates. Test a piece of fabric before applying.

And out of a carpet with nail varnish remover or surgical spirit, then washed gently with warm soapy water.

Nicotine, bicycle and most other oils will come out with carbon tetrachloride and the 'pad at the back' technique. When using carbon tetrachloride or any strong solvent, do so by an open window so that you don't inhale neat fumes.

If a fabric is washable, liquid detergent applied undiluted onto the dry material and worked in first before adding water and rinsing will remove stubborn stains.

Bran or starch sprinkled neat on stains acts on the same principle.

Paint   Fresh emulsion paint is soluble in cold water so if you douse it generously with cold water immediately it's been spilled and then wash in detergent it comes out. If not, a plastic film will form and nothing will budge it.

To remove old and new oil paint marks from a carpet, never use water — this just makes the paint spread out like a halo and then set hard. White spirit (bought from an ironmonger's) dabbed on the stain with a clean paint brush, does the trick. Clean with carbon tetrachloride and a cleaning solvent first until the mark has gone. Only when there is no trace of paint, shampoo with cold or lukewarm carpet shampoo.

Oil paints can be removed from some fabrics — though not all — by sponging with amylacetate (careful, it's inflammable) or turpentine. Don't try to wash until the stain has gone completely, or it will set in forever. Where the stain has hardened, soften it first by putting the solvent on from *underneath* the material whilst holding and renewing the pad on top.

Pencil and coloured crayon marks on woodwork, mock leather and plastic will usually come out with methylated spirit on a pad of cotton wool.

Perspiration   Old stains *won't* come out, but fresh ones should go if soaked in a solution of one part hydrogen peroxide to nine parts water for an hour or so. Then rinse well and wash as usual. This may not be suitable for all fabrics, so test first.

Scorch marks   I'm afraid nothing can be done about a really bad scorch mark — if the fibre's damaged. If it's not too serious, however, and hasn't damaged the threads but still won't come out with normal washing, dampen the stain with water, then soak it in glycerine. After half an hour wash with detergent suds. If the stain's still there, soak for an hour in one part hydrogen peroxide to nine parts water. Finally wash in detergent.

Shoe polish comes off carpets with a spray of spirit spot remover followed by a wipe off.

Tea   Provided the material isn't heat sensitive, run lots of hot water through it to dilute it more and more.

For tea-stains on china — see **China** in the **Cleaning and polishing** section, page 10.

Tomato ketchup   Wash at once in cold water. If there's still a trace, brush a little glycerine into it with a nail brush. Leave for about fifteen minutes, then wash out with warm water and detergent.

Watermarks on woodwork   See **Furniture** in the **Cleaning and polishing** section, page 11.

In the kitchen

Lots of queries and hints I get are naturally concerned with the kitchen — cooking, buying and saving time and money! Money-saving ideas are signalled with a '£' in the margin. Hope you'll find them useful.

Apples   To prevent cooking apples going brown as you peel them, drop prepared apples in a bowl of salted water - one tablespoon salt to a pint of water. Rinse before cooking or using for pie.

Brazil nuts   To crack Brazil nuts and keep them whole, if the shells have become very hard: put the nuts into a saucepan of cold water and bring to the boil. Plunge them again into cold water for a minute or two, drain and leave to dry. The shells will then crack easily and the nuts fall out whole.

£ Bread   Dried or stale bread, especially if home-made, will come up like new if wrapped in a damp cloth for two hours, then placed into a hot oven for ten minutes or so (minus the cloth of course) before the meal.

£ Butter   Make butter go further for parties: beat half a pound of butter with a wooden spoon or in the electric mixer until soft, then gradually blend in two fluid ounces of water. It'll spread more easily as well as going further.

A small knob of butter or marge put into the boiling water with the vegetables discourages a small saucepan from boiling over, but, of course, if you can, use a larger saucepan and turn the heat down.

Cucumber   The lightest sprinkling of castor sugar on slices of cucumber will stop you burping.

Eggs   To cook hard-boiled eggs so they peel easily and don't get that greenish line round the yolk, put them into cold water, bring to the boil, boil for ten minutes, then take them off the stove. Put them immediately in cold water, and change water as soon as it becomes warm.

If you can't remember whether an egg is hard-boiled or not, spin it gently round on its side — a raw one won't spin, a cooked one will.

You can keep fresh eggs in the fridge either raw or hard-boiled for three weeks and they'll taste the same. You can eat them up to several months later, but they won't taste like fresh eggs. Store them pointed end downwards, so that when the yolk rises it touches the air pocket and doesn't stick to the side of the shell.

If you have spare yolks, keep them in a small jar covered with a little cold water to prevent a skin forming. Use them for adding to scrambled eggs, mayonnaise or lemon curd.

Whites left over can be kept covered in the refrigerator until needed. Keep a note of how many are in the container and then use for meringues, adding two ounces of castor sugar for each egg white.

Egg whites whisk more easily if they are at room temperature. Soft-boiled eggs once taken out of the water for a minute or two won't become hard if you start boiling them again.

You can keep poached eggs for a few hours if you leave them immersed in . . . cold water! Just reheat them in hot salted water and they'll come up as good as new!!

Fridge defrosting   When you defrost the fridge keep all the water that drips out — not from the ice-cubes, but the frozen vapour. This is distilled water, and you can use it in your steam iron.

Ice cubes   Those plastic-type trays in chocolate boxes make practical **£** extra ice containers. The 'cubes' come out very easily and in lots of different shapes. As the trays are very brittle you may only be able to use them once, but they are ideal for making attractive ice cubes for a party.

Irish coffee   Here's how you make it. Warm glasses first, pour in a measure of Irish whiskey, add sugar to taste and stir. Leave a spoon in to avoid cracking the glass and add very hot coffee to within half an inch of the top. Stir backwards and forwards and allow to settle. Just before serving, pour in very gently over the back of the spoon thick, unwhipped cream to fill the glass. It must float, not mix, so go really steady.

Jam To help prevent a scum when making jam and jelly, add a good knob of butter when doing the final boil with the sugar. But skim with a large spoon right at the end, otherwise you waste a fair amount of the preserve.

Horseradish sauce When it blows your head off (the freshly scraped nearly always does and some jars are pleasantly potent), bury your nose in a slice of bread and sniff deeply. My Russian grandmother handed this one on to me and it has saved me quite a few blushes.

Kettle care To stop your kettle furring up keep a clean mussel or cockle shell in it. If it has already furred up, quarter fill the kettle and when the water boils, put a heaped teaspoonful of denture powder in it — don't worry, it will fizz up like crazy but won't explode. Leave to cool off, then empty and fill up with clean water again.

There is also on the market a stainless steel wire mesh ball sold especially for kettles. All you have to do is to rub the mesh under a running tap and the white fur flows away down the drain. It prefers to cling to the mesh rather than the kettle.

Lemons Lemons will be twice as juicy if you warm them thoroughly before squeezing.

Lemons are useful to prevent your hands smelling when preparing things like fish, garlic, onions etc. Rub your hands with a slice of lemon *before* you touch them; afterwards, wash hands in cold water, then in soapy water, and then rub them over again with a slice of lemon or with lemon juice.

Lobster If you win the pools and buy a lobster, pick it up. If it smells fresh and the tail snaps back curled under it, it's fresh; if the tail tends to hang down, it's stale.

Meat Cheap cuts of meat will be more tender when cooked if left to marinate an hour or more in a mixture of wine (either red or white), a touch of vinegar, a teaspoonful of finely chopped onion (optional) and mixed herbs — all the better if they're fresh.

Milk To stop milk sticking in an ordinary saucepan, put a little cold water in first — the pan will clean with a wipe instead of a scrape.

A few crushed egg-shells, shaken up vigorously with a little water, will take any milk coating from a glass bottle.

Mint sauce When chopping mint for fresh sauce, two teaspoonsful of sugar on the chopping board makes the job easier. And see the tip for parsley.

Onions For peeling without tears: take off the outer skin but *leave the tufts on at both ends*. Slice in half and place each half downwards with tuft sticking up in the air, then cut across with a very sharp knife — careful not to cut your hand!

Parsley To chop a small amount of parsley quickly, snip small sprigs with kitchen scissors in an old cup or small bowl. You can also do mint in the same way. But a crescent-shaped chopping knife with wooden handles 'rocks' parsley and mint to atoms in seconds.

Rolling pin A glass bottle filled with iced water will make a first-class rolling pin.

Salad When washing salad or other green vegetables, put some salt in the water — any bugs will walk out!

Saucepans Handed down from grandma, but a tip which still prevents a double saucepan from burning: put some marbles in the bottom, then they'll rattle to warn you when the water's running low. If you haven't a double saucepan and just use a single one with a bowl standing inside, this tip still holds.

To clean a badly stained aluminium pan, see the entry on page 10 in the *Cleaning and polishing* section.

£ **Shopping**   You'll usually save money if you buy each supermarket's own brand of products, but it's worth comparing the prices.

£ Because small portions are difficult to find and proportionally more expensive, OAPs – or any other group of single people who live close together – would find it more economical and energy-saving to form a group of six or eight and take it in turn to go shopping. Butter, milk, cheese and even haberdashery items which are easier to buy in larger quantities aren't difficult to divide between friends.

Sinks   If you suffer from a smelly or bunged up kitchen sink: put washing soda in the top of the waste pipe and pour boiling water through. This should at least stop the smell, if not the blockage.

Sourdough   Making sourdough is a waiting game if ever I heard of one, and I'd rather leave it to others, but lots of people have asked me about it so here's how. (Incidentally, I found this recipe for sourdough, which originated in Russia where they call it Balabushky, in an ... American cook book.)

Mix 4 oz plain flour with 8 fluid oz water and 1 tablespoon sugar. Leave in a warm place for three days until fermented. Then sprinkle $\frac{1}{2}$ oz active dry yeast over 12 fluid oz warm water to dissolve and stir into the dough. Add to this mixture 1 lb plain flour, 2 teaspoons salt and 2 teaspoons sugar, then stir vigorously. Place in a greased bowl and cover with a tea towel. Leave for two hours to rise. After it has risen, add $\frac{1}{2}$ teaspoon baking powder, 2 teaspoons salt and 4 oz flour, then stir again. Knead this dough on a board, shape it and put in a greased tin – give it room to grow. Then leave again until it rises this time to double its size. Brush the top with water and score. Pre-heat your oven to 400°F (gas mark 6) and bake for 20 minutes. Then reduce heat to 350°F (gas mark 4) and bake for a further 20–25 minutes. Place a shallow pan of water in the bottom of the oven to prevent the dough from becoming too dry. I wouldn't eat any last thing at night if you haven't got the digestion of an ostrich!!

Spaghetti   Italians prefer to eat their pasta 'al dente' – firm to the tooth – and as cooking times vary according to shape and different makes it's best to test it for just that consistency: all hardness gone, but your teeth mustn't sink too softly through it.

I guarantee spaghetti will never become like wallpapering glue if you follow this Neapolitan tip: after cooking the pasta, drain it, but catch some of the cooking water in a bowl underneath it. Now spread the spaghetti on to a deep dish and slowly ladle some of the cooking water over it. You'll have to gauge the quantity of liquid needed – fork it all around and when the water isn't being absorbed any more, stop. Now add the butter, sauce and so on. Every string will stay separate with no stickiness at all.

Sugar   Why pay extra for castor sugar? All you need do is put granulated sugar into a plastic bag and push the rolling pin over it a couple of times. Better still, if you've got an electric blender reduce the sugar in this. It won't reduce enough to use as icing sugar, but it does make a nice powdery castor sugar.

When granulated sugar has become hard you can treat it in the same way.

If brown sugar hardens, put the packet or container in the fridge and leave it overnight. A large quantity will of course take a bit longer to soften.

Tea   If a packet of tea has been stored next to some soap or disinfectant by mistake and the taste ruined, take a quarter of the peel off a fresh orange and leave it in the tea caddy with the tea. It should be back to its normal flavour next day.

Thermos   The inner tube of a thermos is made of fragile glass which can explode under sharp temperature changes, so cool it with cold running water before pouring in ice-cold drinks and warm it under the hot tap before filling it with boiling hot ones. Don't use a thermos for carrying fizzy drinks.

Tomatoes   The best way to skin tomatoes is to put them in a basin, cover with boiling water and leave for 1–2 minutes until the skin peels easily. Put them in cold water at once, or they will soften with the heat; then peel.

Turkey   How to cook a 14–16 lb turkey in approximately 1½ hours! When I announced I was going to do this (as shown to me by Tony Stoppani, one of Britain's best-known chefs, with a few Royal Banquets to his credit among many other achievements), the family dodged out and stocked up with alternative food for Christmas – they felt our guests mightn't be mad about raw turkey! Now, six or more Christmases later, this method is regarded as the one and only because the bird stays beautifully juicy, and even when cold never goes stringy.
Preheat the oven for about half an hour (gas mark 8, electric 450°) and do not change this heat throughout the cooking. It's vital to keep the same temperature, so watch the Christmas fluctuations and remember that small ovens are likely to overheat.

Stuff the bird in the neck end only and leave the other end empty (I make and serve my chestnut stuffing separately). Pour melted lard over the bird, salt and pepper it and place in the oven. Baste often and cook until, when the baking dish is tilted, the juices inside the turkey run out clear and water-like. *This* is the actual gauge for the cooking time of however large a bird. I found mine, which have varied between 14 and 16 lb, take approximately one and a half hours.

If you have courage to try this way once, you'll feel you've gained a few extra hours of holiday over Christmas.

Flower power

Flowers and plants lighten up the dullest room, but the arranging and caring for them are veritable arts. I have neither the space here nor the knowledge to go into very many details, but there are lots of good paperbacks on the market and you may find there are evening classes in your area on flower arranging. Meanwhile the following hints may come in as useful for you as they do for me.

Flowers in the home

Arranging flowers   Cut the ends of flowers before arranging them so that the stems can continue to absorb water – remember they are alive and need a drink.

Changing the water   Top up or change the water in a vase of flowers as often as you can, cutting a bit from the bottom of the stalks each time.

With flowers such as chrysanthemums, the water won't get smelly if you add a few drops of disinfectant. Hospitals use chlorohexidine.

Cut garden flowers   Always strip off any leaves that would otherwise be under water in a vase. Cut garden flowers should be soaked in a cool dark place in deep water for two hours or overnight and cut in the early morning if the weather is hot and sunny. Use a slant cut and put the flowers up to their necks in tepid water for an hour before arranging.

Woody stems, such as roses and lilacs, should be scraped 2 inches up from the bottom and hammered or squeezed with pliers to help them drink; soak them well before arranging.

The stems of poppies and euphorbias should be singed at the ends over a gas flame or fire.

Hollow stems should be held upside down and filled with water before they are exposed to a warm room. Tepid water is best, as it goes up the stems more quickly.

Dried flowers and leaves   You can dry your own flowers, leaves, grasses, thistles and so on to make very pretty and long-lasting arrangements. Pick them before they are too mature, and hang them upside down in a dry place where the air can circulate. Leave them for a couple of months, then arrange them in a place where they will not get knocked.

Beech leaves preserved with glycerine will last a long time and will look beautiful on their own or with fresh flowers. Split the stems and stand in solution of one part glycerine and two parts hot water – leave for three weeks.

Dried hydrangeas look marvellous arranged in giant clumps—pick the hydrangeas very late in the season and stand in 2 inches of water in a warm place. Let them dry out slowly. This helps them retain their original colour.

Dry rooms   Spray your flower arrangements with water if they're in a very dry room—they'll last longer.

Flower holders   Flower stands as such aren't used much these days; pinholders and plastic foam have taken their place, and of course crumpled chicken-wire is good—though it can leave a rusty mark in your vase.

If you've none of these to hand you can improvise your own stand to put in a bowl or vase: cut a slice from a raw potato large enough for it to rest firmly on the cut side. Then, using a skewer or a long nail, make a few holes to stick the stems into.

Preserving flowers   To keep a bridal bouquet or any other flower for sentimental reasons, sprinkle it generously with borax (available through all chemists)—leave in dry place for 2–3 weeks (until it has dried out). Then keep it in an airtight container, i.e. perspex box sellotaped round the edges.

House plants   Always love to be put out in drizzle or summer rain for a treat.

Dust blocks the pores of leaves and makes them look dull. Either spray or sponge the leaves with clean water—if they've got *very* dusty wipe over carefully with a soft cloth first. Cacti must *never* be washed or sprayed. Use a soft brush to take off the dust.

Proportions   The right proportions are important in every arrangement. You can take it as a general guide that the tallest stem should be $1\frac{1}{2}$ times the height of the vase. This will depend of course on the type of flowers and container—don't be afraid to experiment.

If you're not an expert, you may find that you get the best effect by using an odd number of blooms rather than an even number.

Reviving drooping flowers   This will revive most flowers, especially after a long journey, and is particularly successful with roses and tulips. Snip slantwise an inch or two off each stem, slice about half an inch up the middle of the stems and wrap two or three blooms together quite tightly in a newspaper so they're completely hidden. Now dip the stems into an inch of boiling water for about a minute, not more! Use the egg-timer! Then submerge the flowers completely, still tightly wrapped in the newspaper, in a bath of cold water, and leave for a few hours or overnight if they are very wilted. They'll look wonderful next morning and be all set to arrange. A wilted flower will revive if you float it for two hours in tepid water.

When to cut or buy flowers
Carnations: petals opened but no sign yet of the white stamina.
Chrysanthemums: with tightly curled centre.
Daffodils: buds fully coloured.
Dahlia, double: petals opened but no 'eye' visible.
Gladioli: one or two of the lowest buds should be opening.
Iris: flowers just opening.
Rose: buds but not too tight. (Take off all the thorns.)
Sweet pea: the green shade on the top flowers should be going or gone.
Tulip: tight buds but nearly all coloured.

And here's the odd garden tip for the intermittently keen gardener

Birds can be kept away by placing a single strand of bright red wool over seedlings and cuttings.

Ground cover   If you hate weeding, you won't have to if you use ground cover plants like heather, lily-of-the-valley, cranesbill (geranium), London Pride, saxifrage, pulmoniara, etc.

Plant markers   Lolly sticks make very good plant markers.

Seedling pots   Empty yoghurt pots are very useful to start growing seeds in. Make a hole in the bottom, and they're ideal for cuttings, too. A plastic cover will help them germinate.

Staking Sharp canes used to stake plants can scratch faces and even poke an eye out of someone who bends suddenly when gardening, so cover their tips. Spent cartridge cases or plastic toothbrush cases can be used. Paint them in bright colours so they're clearly visible.

Wire coat-hangers, which are not very good for your clothes, can be useful in the garden. Cut them with pliers, then straighten or shape them as plant supports. Use the tip above to prevent them doing you any damage!

Strips cut from laddered tights make strong 'string' to tie your plants to stakes.

Pets

So you want a pet ...

Pet-owning, to be really successful for both man and beast, must be based on commonsense, thoughtfulness and kindness, not just a vague 'love of animals'. So, if you're thinking of buying a pet, the hints below on buying and caring for animals will give you a good idea of what's involved. Even if you already own a dog or cat, you should find some useful ideas here.

Buying a pet

Take time to choose a pet which will be suitable for your kind of home and way of life — a miniature peke isn't the answer if you've got a houseful of young children or want a dog who'll share your walking holidays, any more than an Afghan hound is right if your idea of exercise is a ten-minute stroll each day. If you're getting a dog as a present for a child, don't buy a toy breed — it's unkind, because most children are instinctively rough. If you insist on giving a pet to a child, make sure that the adult who will in fact have to look after it is willing to do so. With the gift, include a book on the breed or animal (even goldfish and tortoises have their likes and dislikes) plus the whereabouts of the nearest vet.

Now he's yours

When you do get a pet of any kind, take it at once to your vet for a general check-up. Do not put him down on the pavements or into parks before you do this — germs can kill it and the vet will advise you on what inoculations are necessary, and make arrangements for neutering (and I believe

this should be done to all pets unless you seriously intend to breed). Remember, an animal is a living being with feelings, and that you're responsible for it, so buy a book about the right way to take care of your new pet. This will also help you to get the most out of a relationship which, with care, should last for years.

Once you get him home — make him feel at home! Give a dog a bed of his own from the first day he's with you. Make sure it's the right size: when he's fully grown he should be able to sleep in it fully stretched out. Wicker baskets aren't the best things because they're irresistible to chew, aren't draught-proof (an important factor) or very easy to clean. Those collapsible metal-framed beds with canvas sides and bottoms are portable, washable, and come in various sizes — an added cushion and/or blanket will make them more comfortable, but remember to wash these regularly.

A kitten, apart from a bed, must have a litter-tray on his first day in a new home. He'll cotton onto the idea very fast!

From the start make sure a pet always has a bowl of fresh water.

Handle your new pet with care!

Never hold a puppy, kitten or any pet by the scruff of the neck. I know his mother does it, but only when he's very tiny and his weight is negligible. *Never* pick him up by his ears — would you like it? — or by the legs — you could pull them out of their sockets. And *never* hold him clasped round the chest so he can't breathe. The right way to pick him up is like this: *always* put one hand round the side and under him to cup the chest loosely in your palm and the other hand must always support his bottom — this way there's no strain on his spine and he feels secure. If the animal is very small and you are well practised, you can combine this movement with one hand, supporting the bottom on your forearm.

Training your pet

A well-behaved dog is the best of companions, but we've got to teach him with patience how to fit into our lives. A badly behaved pooch is a nuisance to one and all. To have a dog and not to train him is tantamount to cruelty in my opinion. House-training is vital, of course, for everybody's comfort, and walks with your dog will be much more relaxing if he's acquired a proper sense of discipline from an early age. Your own attitude (commonsense and kindness) in this is very important.

Being alone

Get a dog used to the idea that he'll have to stay alone sometimes by leaving him in the kitchen with his bed and toys while you go and do something in another room. A collapsible play-pen is often a useful thing to buy; then your puppy can be left in this with perfect safety.

Words, and above all the tone in which they're said, are as important to dogs as humans — and there's no doubt that a dog who is talked to does become an alert member of the family. Two expressions which work well in partnership are 'Stay — I'm coming back', said reassuringly when you leave a dog alone, and 'I'm back', when you put the key in the door. Quite soon, when he hears the first, although obviously disappointed, he'll go quietly to his bed, and will greet 'I'm back' with wild enthusiasm.

Cats and furniture

Cats *can* be trained not to sharpen their claws on furniture. Get a thick round log about 3 feet long with the bark still on it if possible, and cover half of it with cheap velvet. Then every time the cat makes for the best armchair, tap him firmly with a rolled newspaper and redirect him to his own scratching ground. That look of indifference is disdain, and far from stupidity. He'll eventually fall in with the house rules . . . if you insist.

House-training

Cats are naturally clean and if you show your kitten his litter tray and make it clear what it's for, he'll use it in preference to making a mess.

Puppies take a little longer to learn, however. Most pups come from breeders with the rough idea that newspaper is for penny spending, so allot a special corner of the kitchen or cloakroom for this — keep a newspaper down and a free way to it always, so he has no excuse to make a mistake.

When house-training a puppy, and especially a male one (they have smaller bladders than bitches) remember to take him to his paper or outside every half hour or so, and do this the moment he wakes up and straight after he's had something to eat.

It's a good idea to repeat the *same* words of encouragement each time: such as 'spend a penny', 'tinkle', or what you will. Praise him lavishly when he obliges and he'll soon catch on, because it's a fact that animals prefer to be clean. If he makes a mistake, don't rub his nose in the puddle, it's quite unnecessary — a gruff tone of voice will give him the message.

If you've been so successful at paper training a pup that when he's outside he'll hold everything until he gets back indoors, he'll soon get the idea that it's OK outside too if you put a sheet of newspaper in the gutter and say those same magic words a few times.

It's not a bad idea, especially if you live in a flat, to keep a small dog paper-trained for the early morning and late night pennies. It's more comfortable for the animal, and you won't have to brave the elements. If you have a long-haired bitch, pat her dry afterwards with a bit of loo paper — it's cleaner for her and your home.

Making friends

Once a puppy has had his anti-distemper innoculation, let him be friendly with other dogs — if you pull him away or lift him up he could sense fear through you and turn into a fighter.

Praise and punishment

Animals have a great sense of fairness, so won't resent being scolded when they've done something wrong, but they need and thrive on praise, too, when they've tried to please. For instance, when you call a dog and he takes no notice at first, but eventually comes slinking up to your repeated calls, *don't hit him* — if you do he's even less likely to obey you next time. Instead, reassure him with a gentle pat because he did, if belatedly, come to you. Authority, plus a firm attitude of mind, is essential. It's no good saying 'You bad dog' in the same sweet tone that you'd croon 'What a good boy'. When you want him to know you're mad, make sure you sound mad. And again, don't plead 'Come here' — make it an order. You may think I'm stating the obvious, but I've heard this mistake made time and time again by women who add (not unexpectedly), 'My dog won't do a thing I tell him.'

Never hit an animal with a hard stick or even your hand, because you could injure him internally. A tap with a rolled up newspaper is very effective. The best 'tapping' areas are the buttocks. Never hit him hard on the nose or about the head — think again of the possible internal injury.

Toys

When training a pup, give him his own toys in preference to your slippers —

those beef-hide chews in different shapes and sizes will help him to cut his teeth, keep them clean and even when he's older will keep him amused for hours.

Walking

When training a puppy to walk on a lead, don't pull him: encourage him, get him interested in something ahead of him—hold either a toy or his ball, and he'll forget he's tethered to you. Reward him with a stroke and a dog choc-drop.

To encourage a dog to walk to heel, hold him on a shortish lead and repeat the word 'Heel'. If he keeps easing forward, tap him very lightly on the nose with a rolled newspaper (which won't hurt him). Praise him when he gets the idea, but never lose your temper, even if he's slow to learn. Patience is vital when training any animal.

Never *chase* a disobedient dog—he'll think it's a game and keep going. Instead, walk or run away from him and pretend not to look back. This usually works because all dogs are scared of being lost. If he still won't come and you eventually have to catch him on the run, give him a few sharp swishes on the backside with a tightly rolled newspaper or a light birch (these are good when a big dog's a problem puppy because that swishing sound they make is often as effective as the feel of them), tell him firmly he's very wicked, and keep him on the lead for the rest of the walk.

Caring for your pet

Be kind and thoughtful to your animal! Of course, it goes without saying that you don't want to be unkind to your pet, but sometimes we don't realise that we are—and of course, he can't tell us.

For instance, it's always kinder to stroke an animal, rather than pat it. Pats are nerve-jangling. If you don't believe me, watch how even a hefty horse or a hound blinks under a hearty pat.

It's also cruel to make a small dog walk along a crowded street—just put yourself in his place. How would you feel, if you were helplessly surrounded by a moving forest of gigantic legs and shoes? The best answer to this is to train your small dog to hop into an egg basket. (A flat, washable cushion covered with a small towel will make it comfortable.) Then after

a walk, he'll jump in, you can loop the handle over your arm and set off shopping. It's much easier than carrying him, and your clothes won't get covered with dog hairs or dirty on a wet day. What's more, wherever you take him he'll feel secure because he's got a home from home. Choose an egg basket because the way the handle is attached on most other baskets makes the balance such that the dog may topple out if he moves.

Never grab any animal from behind—a dog could instinctively snap out of fear and in self-defence. Call him and let him see what you're up to before you touch him.

Never leave an animal in a car on a hot day, even with the windows open—remember that even on a warm day the inside of a car gets uncomfortably hot. You might come back to find him dead from a heart attack or heatstroke, and think of the panic and pain he'll have gone through.

Cleaning and bathing

Clean your dog's face, mouth and eyes either with a mild disinfectant generously diluted with warm water on a pad of cotton wool, or on a wrung-out cooled-off tea bag. Cats, of course, prefer to work on themselves.

To keep a long-haired dog clean and above all dust-free in a town, wipe him over thoroughly every evening with a damp cloth or flannel (kept clean and especially for this purpose) wrung out in hot water laced with bayrum (a generous sprinkling of spirit-based bayrum in a washing-up bowl of water), followed with a quick rough towel-dry and brush. This will check any doggy smell.

When bathing a dog, start from the tail and work upwards. Head last, and don't get any water in the ears. It's a good idea to wash the face separately before the bath, and smear a little eye ointment round the eyes to help keep out the soap. Dry him thoroughly (a hair-dryer helps), and don't let him go out for at least two hours after a bath. In the winter, it's best to wash them very last thing at night after they've spent their last penny. Some vinegar (amount according to size of animal) in the last rinsing water helps the comb-through, and gives a good shine to the coat. A hair conditioner also works on long-haired dogs.

Collars and harnesses

Although some schools of thought hold with slip-chain collars, I don't, because I know of a number of accidents caused through them, in particular the case of a very sensible airedale who got hooked up on barbed wire, panicked, got badly gashed and strangled himself into the bargain. If, in your own mind, you're master of your dog and firm with him, a normal leather or rolled collar with your name and address on it is the answer.

Pekes and pugs should always wear harnesses—they have difficulty enough in breathing without the added pull on their wind-pipe. Apart from that, their necks are nearly as broad as their heads, so it's quite easy for them to slip a collar. Any small dog who tends to fight is easier to hoick up out of trouble if he's wearing a harness.

If you have a tiny dog do choose a light lead with a small clip—a heavy one will clonk against its head and hurt.

Feeding hints

Ask your vet's advice on which food and how much to give your pet. I know someone who gave a large growing Afghan hound only one tin of dog food, or one sachet of dried meat a day because it was described as 'complete food', then wondered why the pooch was listless. Poor dog, it was starving. It's a fact that slimmer animals live longer and healthier lives, but they have to be well nourished.

When giving your dog a bone, make sure it's always a *beef* knuckle or shin bone—never chicken or lamb (no, *not even a leg of lamb*). These can splinter and easily pierce the intestine.

Raw vegetables such as carrots, spinach and cabbage, either grated or whole, are excellent for dogs. They contain natural chlorophyl which helps to curb doggy smells. But *no* lettuce—this gives them gripes.

Keep two bowls specially for your pet, one for his food and one for his water. Choose bowls which have a wider base than top – even rough puppy paws find those difficult to upset.

Remember that bowl of ever-fresh water.

Never feed your pet from the table, even though that soulful stare can be very unnerving. Give him his food first and then make him sit quietly in a corner while you have your meals.

Friends and foes

Do be thoughtful to other dog-owners. If your dog is a fighter he should of course be kept on a lead if you can't rely on his obedience. But even if yours is just a large, over-friendly animal, train him not to be rough with small breeds because, even in play, he could easily break a back or brain a little dog. Then again, if you have a small animal, play safe and give a wide berth to large boisterous dogs who are obviously enjoying a game.

Health hints

If a pet goes off his food, particularly a very young one, there's usually something wrong. Don't wait for him to get really really ill before taking him to the vet.

Never give a cat aspirin or any derivative of this, because it can poison him. It's not quite so lethal for dogs, but in the case of all pills it's wiser to consult a vet.

If a dog's ears are hot, and certainly if he keeps scratching them or hanging his head to one side, he's probably got a touch of canker. Don't probe into an animal's ears yourself – a vet must deal with canker, and quickly. It hurts a lot, so if a child grabs a dog's ear, even an angelic-natured animal might snap out of pain.

If a dog keeps nibbling his paws and chasing his tail, he probably needs worming – consult the vet.

Keep an eye on nails. City dogs in particular should have theirs clipped occasionally; some walk flat-footed on pavements and a nail can curl under and grow into the pads. Stay-at-home cats, too, can have their claws blunted by the vet.

Take the trouble to dry a dog after a walk in the rain, and always dry wet paws. This will avoid painful rheumatism in his old age.

Never let a pup pull on string when he's playing; it could cut into his gums and mouth. Use a thick cord or a rag. Don't swing him off his feet: he could let go and be hurled into something, or lose a tooth or two.

Flat-faced dogs sometimes need an inhalent to de-block their noses. Friars Balsam is excellent, and so is bicarbonate of soda sprinkled over boiling hot water. Sit on the floor with the dog between your legs, make him sit and hold his shoulders so his head is over the bowl and he can inhale comfortably. The bicarbonate should be fizzing.

Travel and holidays

It's wisest not to get a dog, or any other pet for that matter, unless you have a willing family or reliable friend who'll be happy to look after him, especially if you holiday abroad. If you have to send him to a boarding kennel, remember these do vary tremendously, so take the trouble to inspect personally the one you choose before leaving your pet there. If the people are reluctant to show you around, go elsewhere. You can get a list of boarding kennels from your local town hall or public library. A boarding kennel should be licenced by the local authority; if it isn't, this could mean that the owners can prove another source of main income and are taking in animals only as a profitable side-line with no experience and little regard for their welfare.

If you holiday in the British Isles, remember that your dog loves a change too, so include him in your plans. It's at times like these that sensible training will pay dividends in full. A booklet called *Pets Welcome* (available at most book-stalls) gives a list of hotels and boarding houses where you can take your pet.

When travelling with any animal, particularly on a warm day, take a container of water with you – he'll get as thirsty as you do. If your pet is obviously feeling the heat, put some water on its head and keep it damp. And, as I said before, please don't cause him unnecessary suffering by keeping him in a car on a hot day.

Quarantine

It's really not worth taking an animal abroad, as dogs and cats must have an import licence to be brought into Britain, and spend six months in quarantine kennels from the date when they arrive, in case they should be incubating rabies.

Fashion
Making the most of yourself

There's no secret to good grooming—just a very active needle, cotton, clothes brush, shoe polishing, etc etc, plus lots of soap and water and a constant, scrupulous attention to all details, from hair to heels, and that includes hems.

The basic fashion rule is to *know yourself*. Take stock of your figure with neither false modesty nor rose-tinted glasses. Then you can always adapt today's fashions to suit yourself. Proportions are important to the overall effect of clothes, so a full-length looking glass is a must. Make sure it's an 'honest' one—neither slimming nor fattening. If you can't find a 'tryptic' (a full-length mirror with two mobile sides of the same size attached) place two large looking glasses in such a way that you can get a full length front and back and side view of yourself. A bit of manoeuvring pays dividends all round (and mirrors always make rooms appear larger!).

Don't let measurements fool you. It doesn't matter so much what a woman's measurements are as how they are distributed—two women can have a 37 inch bust but look totally different if one has a broad back and the other carries all before her. The same goes for two ladies with 38 inch hips. The first may have a broad pelvis, whilst the other can boast a rounded bottom! So look in that mirror.

Incidentally, a buxom bottom will look less so if skirts are cut on the cross.

Don't worry if you're not conventionally pretty, pick out a too 'definite' feature which you may be tempted to play down, and make the most of it—for instance, a very wide mouth, a widow's peak hairline, an extra skinny figure, or a giraffe-like neck—whatever it is, turn it into a trump card, then you will stand out and score over the many a pretty, pretty girl. I am sure I need not add that you must make the most of your good features too—such as accentuate a slim waist with a chic belt, and well-shaped hands with unusual rings.

If you do have figure problems, face them. Don't yen to be a tailored type when your sloping Victorian shoulders can make you an ultra-feminine knock-out. Fashions change too much to be specific but play along with soft wools, silks and all those flatteringly flowing man-made fabrics—rule out all 'stiff' versions of silks or tweeds.

Equally, if your shoulders are frankly square, make the most of what can be turned into a casual sophisticated look. Chanel style suits are for you — smart leather belts and beautiful bags with matching shoes should be your extravagances. You can carry important jewellery, chunky gold bracelets with one large medallion. For the evening you will look smashing in a full-length shirt waister dress. The shirt waister style makes a very attractive evening dress when you give it added glamour by using such materials as velvet, lamé, lace and satin.

If you're BIG be BOLD. Walk tall in mind and body. Choose important looking clothes — capes and bright patterns won't swamp you, and there are plenty of men who believe the bigger the better. One big DON'T: don't ever wear your skirts too short. The proportions will be all wrong and kill your natural presence.

Anyone with a stumpy neck should avoid all rounded necklines, especially those that dip at the back of the neck as well as the front. They accentuate the stumpiness, and from the side view — unless a woman is as straight as a ramrod from neck to waist — they'll add ten years to her age. Alternatives are 'V' necklines with a small turn-back collar and plunge oblongs, still with a turn-back collar — that 'bare' line always seems to be fattening. And for the evenings, make sure that a décolleté ends in a 'sharp' plunge and not a rounded one.

A big bust will look bustier in very high waisted clothes and smock styles. With a big bust, unless you want to look like a nursing mother when dressed, you have to wear a bra which *keeps* that well-divided look. The French manufacturers have the answer which is usually a light semi-circle of wire under each cup but try before you buy.

If your legs could be a bit longer watch that hemline. If the midi is in, shorten it a fraction (consult that full-length looking glass for how much). And although high heels are helpful, exaggeratedly high ones defeat their object and draw attention to any lack of leg length.

If you're broad on top with plump arms don't kid yourself that raglan sleeves will camouflage the fact — set-in sleeves are kinder. Always beware of clinging jersey-type materials.

Whatever your problems and/or assets be realistic. A dress that looks superb in a shop window or on your best friend may not suit you; a vibrant, zinging colour may look lovely on its own, but it may detract from your own complexion or hair-colour.

Read fashion magazines. The really glossy ones with out of reach prices are the ones to look at and get the 'feel' of design for today's scene. It will prevent us from being dull in our more realistic choice of clothes. It is the little ideas such as a scarf tied differently or a sudden splash of un-expectedly complementary colours that spell 'chic'.

In the fitting room, transport yourself in mind and feeling back home. Tune your imagination and you will learn whether the choice will be a success with family and friends.

When buying a hat remember that overall proportions are very important so never try on a hat sitting down or without a full-length mirror and of course never choose a picture hat when wearing tweeds and flat shoes or a racing hat when you have been to a garden party.

If you wear your hair long and straight make sure there's a 'break' in the line between locks and shoulder or you'll look neck-less. (Those full-length proportions will have gone for six again.)

Face that candid camera

You won't be self-conscious if you see the lens as the face of a friend you know well. Smile and 'say' something to him or her—the result will be natural and if serious still keep talking to that . . . friendly lens.

If you have difficulty in smiling naturally—never say cheese if asked to smile—tuck the tip of your tongue behind your top front teeth instead— you'll hold a normal grin.

Wear either white or a pastel shade near your face—it's more flattering to your skin in a photograph. Dark colours call for different lighting and your face will come off second best.

Never stand square on to a camera — a slight swivel to the left or the right sheds the odd pound in the print.

If in doubt whether to add another bauble or bangle—DON'T. It's a good everyday rule this, but the camera will exaggerate any clutter.

Making the most of your clothes

Making the most of yourself of course includes making the most of the clothes you've already got, and I've collected the following hints on clothes care—ironing, washing, alterations, and so on.

Caring for your clothes

Belts   If you've lost the loop of a belt and the end flops untidily, either glue or sew a strip of Velcro to the underneath of the flopping bit, and another to the part of the belt where it should rest. You'll have no more trouble.

Boots and shoes   Back copies of magazines, tightly rolled (yes, even the *TVTimes*), make economical boot-shapers.

Scuff marks will usually come off boots and shoes if first wiped clean, then dried and then rubbed firmly with a slice of raw onion.

White spirit or methylated spirit will usually clean up white wet-look boots and shoes—but once I've wiped off dark dirt streaks with that slice of raw onion.

Bras   If you haven't burnt your bra, it'll fit better and make the most of what you've got if you bend over and let your breasts fall into it when you put it on, *then* stand up and fasten it.

Underwear   When wearing white or pastel tops, a beige or skin-tone bra will be hardly noticeable.

Never put even a slightly boned bra into the washing machine.

Chiffon   A tip from the royal wardrobes: to clean chiffon, rub the material with very little damp soap, then place a pad of cotton wool under the mark and put a slice of lemon on top of it—leave it like that for about half an hour. Soak the marked chiffon in a little luke-warm salted water and watch the progress, or rather the regression, of the stain. Finally rinse carefully in salt-free water.

Clothes brush   If you've lost yours, a good substitute is sticky tape wound round the palm of your hand, sticky side out, and patted over the material.

For clothes which smell musty even after they've been washed, wash them again and shake some inexpensive bath cologne into the final rinse. Let them soak for a few minutes. Spin-dry them apart from other clothes, or better still, dry them out of doors.

Crêpes and certain other man-made fabrics should always be ironed on the wrong side or with a damp cloth, to prevent them shining.

Dry cleaning   Methods are improving all the time, and it does prolong the life and looks of clothes, because dirt settling into clothes literally eats into the fabric. I've heard it said that there are between $2\frac{1}{2}$ and 3 ounces of dirt and oily remnants in an average suit going to the cleaner's—that's equivalent to a handful of small change, or the weight of a full packet of cigarettes. Ugh! But make sure the dry cleaner belongs to the Association of Launderers and Dry Cleaners (see address at the back of the book).

Dyeing   If you want to dye clothes or fabrics (and it's often well worth-while) make sure they're in good condition. If they're worn, dyeing won't wave a wand and renew them, and most dyeing is undertaken at your own peril!

Electric?   If you crackle when taking off your clothes, or they stick to you, buy anti-static underclothes—more and more chain stores sell them. And when washing, give all synthetic clothes and underwear a final rinse through in one of the excellent fabric conditioners.

Fur   To clean fur and fun-fur collars, cuffs and cravats, give them a dry-oatmeal or bran shampoo. Heat a pound or so of oatmeal in a very low oven, then rub handfuls of it well into the fur. Massage it in and leave it a while. Shake it out and do it again with some fresh oatmeal. A final brush and the fur will look and feel revitalised.

Girdles   If you like the support of a panti-girdle but loathe the roll it pushes up above the waist, buy a size larger than you need to. You can always snip off the tell-tale tag. It doesn't defeat its purpose. But you should be exercising your muscles into forming a natural girdle (see the section on Beauty).

Hanging your clothes up   Never hang them in the wardrobe still warm from your body. They need to breathe a bit first, otherwise the material as well as the cupboard will take on a musty smell.

The sharp edges of wire coat hangers aren't too kind to clothes. Padded ones are best for dresses, while wooden—though not exaggeratedly hunch-back—hangers keep suits in good shape.

Hats   Hard-brimmed straw hats once dented have to be professionally re-blocked so they should be kept carefully with the crown stuffed with tissue paper in a large hat box or boxes which will neither crush nor cramp them.

Heavy fabrics, such as trousers and suits, should always be pressed with a damp cloth.

Jeans and trousers   If you're not a good presser, run a row of tacking stitches up the front crease of each leg before washing jeans or trousers; then all you do is line up the stitches and your creases will be in the right place when you iron them. Use silk thread rather than cotton so it won't mark the material under the hot iron. This works when ironing pleated skirts too.

Let clothes rest   Don't wear the same ones day after day, and they'll give you much longer service. The same goes for shoes.

Man-made fibres Never dry clothes in man-made fibres out in the glaring sunshine because they can develop rust-like marks which just won't come out.

Nylon Nylon fur hats can be washed by swishing the outside of them around in Stergene according to the instructions. Help the dirt off with a nail brush, but keep the inside of the hat as dry as possible. It'll help if you can pull the lining out and hold it in your (dry) hand. After a final rinse a dunk in fabric softener will soften the fabric. Don't wring, but cover the hat with a bath towel and press out the water. Set the hat smoothly over a wig block to dry. A hand-drier and comb-out will speed up this process and help the lining to dry that much quicker too if it's become wet.

White nylon and most other synthetic fibres can be re-whitened if you soak them in a detergent with the correct amount of bleach blended in – never use bleach alone on them. The best way to keep them white is to wash each garment after every wearing with simple soap.

Ostrich feathers (These will always be flatteringly feminine.) Should you have to dye them (we did for my dress in the last Eurovision Song Contest I introduced) start off with white feathers and use Dylon. Follow the mixing instructions carefully but watch the feathers as they change colour, so you can fish them out when you think right (they'll dry approximately four shades lighter than they look wet). Don't despair as you stir (with a wooden spoon) the ostrich feather soup, and don't panic when you fish out a tatty bit of string. Shake it thoroughly (outside if possible – mind the walls), then hang a plastic sheet over a clothes-horse and drape the pathetic offering over it. Now get to work gently with a hair-dryer and wide-toothed comb – the scene soon changes, and you can put an extra curl into the feathers with a tail comb as you dry.

Patent leather can be polished beautifully with spray-on furniture polish. (And remember most marks on patent come out with a touch of methylated spirit.)

Hair spray and ball-point pen marks will come off with methylated spirit on a pad of cotton wool. Meths is always worth trying to get off any mark on this surface.

Pigskin To clean a not-too-dirty pigskin coat or jacket (if it's got too dirty have it done professionally) go over it first with a stiff bristle clothes or rubber brush, then lay a sheet of thick brown wrapping paper on it, shiny side up, and iron over it with a hot iron.

Pleated skirts See tip under **Jeans and trousers.**

Rainwear should be dry-cleaned regularly and reproofed at the same time. Don't let it get too dirty, or that grubby look will never go, even after cleaning. The old-fashioned riding mackintosh has to be scrubbed with soap and warm water, then left to dry away from direct heat.

Shiny suits Even a new suit will shine if you run a hot iron directly onto the cloth, but you can dull it down again if you place a clean, *dry* towel on the shiny surface with another damp one on top of it, then press with a hot iron. This trick can sometimes dull the shine of an aging suit, and a steam iron makes the job easier.

Shoes See my tips in **Boots and shoes** above.

Spectacles Methylated spirit on a pad of cotton wool will get spectacle rims clean (the glass too). Rinse them well under cold running water and dry with a clean cloth.

Stains There's a whole section dealing with stain removal in the HOUSEHOLD section, pages 13–16. Remember, if in doubt, take the garment along to the dry cleaner's and tell them what the stain is.

Suede can be freshened up by rubbing with a piece of crêpe soling – a clean piece, of course. Don't use the sole of your walking shoes!

Tights It's important to shop around for tights which really fit well – if they're too small the fibres will be stretched tight and will snap easily, and if they're too large they'll be loose and catch on things.

To get the best wear from tights, never wear them more than once without washing them. Sitting down to take them on and off and if your hands and nails aren't satin smooth wear gloves. Handle them in or out of the wash as little as possible.

To camouflage ugly veins on legs wear a pair of white tights with an ordinary shade of tights on top. In the case of support stockings choose the palest shade possible, then slip a pair of darker tights over them. And to avoid problems make doubly sure to buy the right foot size.

Under-arm shields do protect dresses from perspiration. Don't sew them in: fix them with a series of strategically placed press-studs. They'll be easier to take out and wash and you won't need so many pairs.

Velvet can be successfully pressed face down on a terry towel. But don't lean too heavily on the iron, because once velvet fibres have been broken nothing can repair them.

Velvet brushes up well with a square of dressmaking canvas.

Don't try reviving velvet over a steaming kettle – this outdated method only scalds fingers and frays tempers. Instead, lay a damp cloth on the velvet pile side up, then *skim* a really hot iron along it, but don't let the iron actually rest on the cloth. The pile will perk up towards the heat.

Specks and fluff on velvet will come off if the velvet is dusted with a crumpled ball of stiff milliner's canvas.

Woollies Take one large packet of soap-flakes and put it into a screwtop jar, add one breakfast cup of methylated spirits and three dessertspoonsful of eucalyptus oil. Screw down well. When required, put one tablespoonful of this into a bowl of warm water and squeeze woollies in this. If very dirty, change the water and start again with another tablespoonful. When the garment is washed in this way there is no need to rinse it because the methylated spirit dissolves the soap-flakes and the eucalyptus oil restores natural oil to the wool. This is an old German washing method.
So long as a cardigan or jumper isn't too heavy and likely to hang out of shape, this is a good way to dry it after washing. Put it on a hanger inside an open-ended plastic cover from the dry cleaner's. Then peg the hanger's hook on the clothes line where it can be left out overnight without fear of it getting spotted or rained on.

Alterations

Fur If you're brave enough to do alterations in fur, use a razor blade to cut it along the skin side only, never snip through the fur itself. Fur should be sewn by over-sewing, edge to edge.

Hems Wide sticky tape will level a dropped hem in an emergency more smoothly than safety pins.

A solvent which will take out some glue stains – though not all, unfortunately Copydex for instance – is used as follows. Take two generously sized pads of cotton wool, soak one in amylacetate and put it underneath the material, whilst holding the other dry pad on top of the stain. Keep dabbing the underside of the stain, and it should transfer from the material to the cotton wool on top. Finally, wash in the usual way. *Warning:* try out the solvent on a hidden part of the material first to make sure it doesn't affect either the fabric or the dye.

Before lengthening a hem, check whether the colour is worn away at the hemline; this often happens with clothes that shrink after washing a lot, and will leave a permanently faded line. With a generous hem you can cover the faded line mark with braid, velvet, or leather.

If there's no fade mark, lengthening a hem will still leave a darker looking line where the original hemline was. White spirit will usually get this out of white and other light-coloured trousers or skirts.

But tackle the actual crease line of a hem like this: soak a strip of heavy dressmaking canvas in water (you may have to buy half a yard and cut it), then place the wet strip over the raised edge of the let-down hem, cover it with a cloth and press with a hot iron until the canvas is dry. Now take hold of the hem and pinch it *across* the way it runs, bend it back on itself and generally work it in all directions except the original one in which it lay. After this, wet the canvas and do it all over again. Two or three complete cycles usually smooth out the tell-tale line.

Never try to iron out the hem crease in velvet without looking to see if the material has been broken. If it has, don't bother. If it's a brand-new dress you want to lengthen, look at the velvet under a magnifying glass. If the fibres are intact go ahead and iron as per suggestions.

Don't try to iron out any materials with permanent pleatings which have been 'cooked' in, such as drip-dry trouser creases.

Sewing and knitting tips

Buttonholes   Loosely woven fabric won't fray when making a button-hole if you paint both sides of the material first with a thin line of colourless nail varnish and leave to dry before cutting inside the linen.

Buttons   A button will stay on more firmly if you paint the holes with a colourless nail varnish, or even a touch of glue, just before you sew it on. As you sew, it will coat the thread and strengthen it.

Children's wear and tear   If children always go through the knees of their trousers first, prevent this by buying half a yard of 2-inch iron-on tape each time you buy a new pair. Cut the tape into four pieces (two for each leg) and iron the pieces onto the inside of the trousers at the knees. The trousers will last months longer.

Cotton   Reels of cotton won't disappear if threaded through a piece of close-knit covering wire, cut into a circle or rectangle to fit the shape of your workbox. The thread can then be snipped off without taking the reels out of the box.

Knitting   If you're knitting with several coloured balls of wool, thread each colour through a different hole in a colander. The wools won't tangle and the colander can be used as a temporary knitting basket.

Needles   To thread a darning needle quickly when the wool is thick, fold a short piece of cotton in two and push the wool through the loop formed. Thread the two ends of cotton through the needle's eye, pull gently, and the wool strand will follow.

Pockets   Cast-off nylon shirts can be used to repair worn pockets in teenagers' trousers or jackets. Snip out the old pocket, lay it on the back panel of the shirt and use it as a pattern for size and shape of the new one. If there's enough shirt material make the new pocket in double thickness — it will last longer.

Soft toys   If you make soft toys or have a friend who does, save worn tights for stuffing — they're far cheaper than kapok.

A hold-all   Don't throw out that favourite old sweater. Just cut off the top and the sleeves, sew up the bottom and the sides and attach to a bag frame. Line it for extra strength, and you'll have a very personal 'hold-all'.

Zips   To put in a zip, sew up the seam opening with tacking stitches, stitch the closed zip in position over the seam, then remove the tacking stitches.

When the babies have grown out of nappies, keep the pins. Then, when the knitting pattern tells you to 'leave so many stitches on needle' you can slip them onto the nappy pin and they won't slide off.

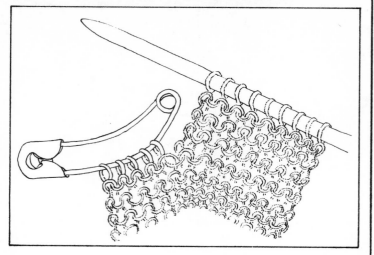

Some unusual ideas

A hair slide can be given a new look by gluing two or three important-looking buttons on top. Gilt or silver are the most effective—small ones just look titchy.

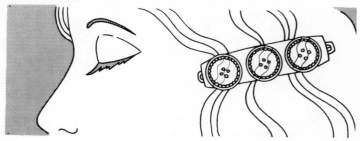

Necklaces To make an effective, economical and very individual necklace, slide a belt buckle (one or more according to taste) onto a ribbon (width according to taste *and* neck length). Cut and fasten to the right size with either a bow or a small strip of Velcro.

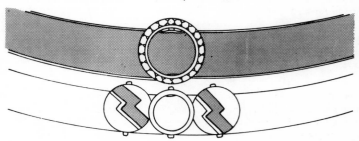

Rings If you like wearing different rings have your wedding ring made half in red gold and half in white—then a twiddle will keep it in colour with your other ring settings.

A bikini wrap One and three-quarter yards of drip-dry cotton, 36 inches wide and hemmed narrowly, will pack flat and twist into several shapes as a lunchtime wrap over bikinis. It'll double as a holiday dressing gown, too. A cool and effective material is patterned voile — sale remnants come in handy.

A bikini bra strip — as sketched — just a straight length of material.

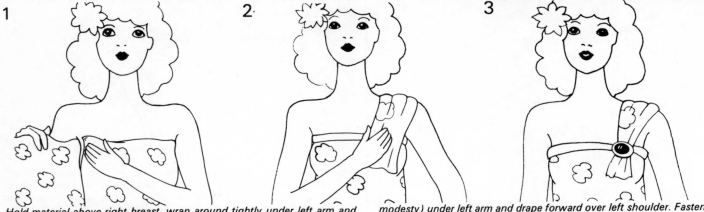

Hold material above right breast, wrap around tightly under left arm and bring forward under right arm. Pass across front again (in the name of modesty) under left arm and drape forward over left shoulder. Fasten with brooch. Secure over right breast with unseen safety pin or tuck under.

Bring forward strip of material from the back — tie in a knot — work flatteringly over the bust and tuck in loose ends.

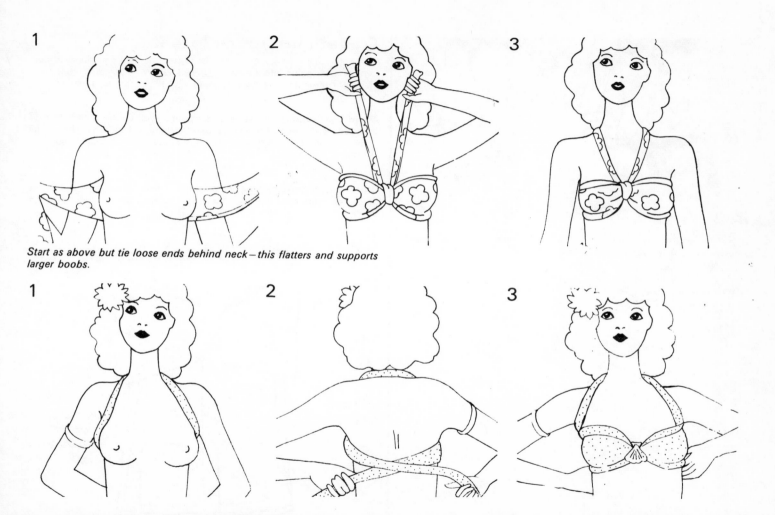

1

2

3

Start as above but tie loose ends behind neck — this flatters and supports larger boobs.

1

2

3

Use a slimmer and longer piece of material — start at the back of neck — bring forward and take back under the arms — cross over behind, bring for-ward again and drape over bust — tie with knot and tuck in the ends — brooch optional.

39

Wrap this round higher or lower on your waist according to your figure to go with the three bra tops on the previous pages.

Travel and your clothes

Aerosols It's explosively dangerous to pack aerosol containers in luggage which is going into the unpressurised hold of an aeroplane, but quite OK to put them in hand-baggage carried in the pressurised cabin.

Avoid last-minute pressure and panic Well before departure date start two lists on large sheets of paper. On number 1 jot down things still to do, on number 2 things you're going to pack. You can add or subtract as you go along.

Clothes won't crease if, when packing, you use masses of plastic sheets (keep the bags returned from the dry cleaner's) as you would tissue paper.

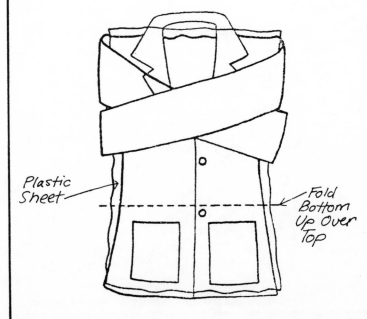

Plastic Sheet

Fold Bottom Up Over Top

On all my travels I have never known the 'plastic-packed' clothes to crease more than a little, but should this happen, fill the bath with really hot water, hang the clothes in the bathroom and close the door so that the steam gets to work on them. Half an hour should do the trick. Then bring them out and if possible hang them in a draught to dry them off.

A collapsible bag packed at the bottom of your suitcase will be very useful for things you'll collect on the way.

Hard suitcases should be packed with flat heavy things and shoes first.

Labelling   Lots of suitcases look alike, so cross yours with coloured sticky tape, or tape your initials on the side to make it instantly recognisable.

Snappy plastic bags are invaluable for that bikini still damp after the last swim, that just-started bottle of tanning oil you can't throw out but which might leak, those still-sandy sandals, etc.

Soft-surfaced suitcases need a protective bottom as well as top layer of clothes, otherwise when closed any sharp edges will put a strain on the surface. All cases should be packed on the tight side, but especially soft-surfaced ones, or clothes will arrive very journey-jaded.

Health and beauty
Health

Beauty and health go hand in hand because how we look depends very much on how we feel inside. That's why I've started off this chapter with a section especially about health.

There's plenty of information here on general health, foot care, herbs, vitamins as well as that great method of relaxation, Yoga – all of which should help you to feel good. First of all, though, there are some tips on caring for your back which is where so many of our aches and pains start.

Caring for your back

Exercise   All exercise is really based on breathing and stretching. Remember – you're as young as your spine is supple and Yoga can help to keep this so. But when you're doing the housework – yes, making the beds, dusting, sweeping, washing the kitchen floor and so on – stretch out, pull in your tummy, and look on the whole thing as beauty therapy. If it's in the mind, then it'll help the body, too!

This is a very good Yoga style exercise for loosening up the spine and getting rid of that painful ache that can grip across the shoulders. Stand up, let your arms hang loosely by your sides, then slowly move both shoulders up and back in a slow shrug whilst breathing in. Bring them down forward, and breathe out. Up and back again in a continuous circular movement. You should feel the movement in the small of your back and a tingle up the spine. Repeat four times. Now reverse the whole movement four times: go forward, down, back and up. Finally, rotate each shoulder separately, also four times. Bring the *right* shoulder up, in the same smooth circular movement, then back, down, forward, up and back again, *at the same time* bringing the *left* shoulder down, forward, back up and forward again. This simultaneous movement of the shoulders rotates the bones of the spine in their sockets so the vertebrae are gently and very slightly twisted from side to side. It's very important to let the arms hang loosely all the time and just let them go along with the shoulders as they move. I find it also helps to have a mental image of the vertebrae rotating and loosening up.

Hanging curtains When hanging up or taking down heavy curtains, push them behind you and rest the main bulk on your shoulders, so they'll take the weight and avert the risk of back trouble.

Sneezing Don't turn your head to the side to sneeze—you could rick a disc. As you sneeze aim dead straight ahead (yes, a hankie would be sociable) and bend at the knees—this will ensure that your spine isn't jarred.

Wash basin height If you do have a say when the builders install the wash basins, remember to have them placed at the right height. This is one of those tiny details that make life more comfortable.

If you're stuck with a basin that is much too low for you, however, as often happens, bend your knees when you sloosh your face and clean your teeth. It'll be more comfortable, especially first thing in the morning.

Picking things up When you pick something up from the floor, always *bend at the knees*. If you just bend over from the waist you could rick your back.

General health tips

Arthritis   This remedy may be considered an old wives' tale by some, but I've seen my grandmother's very arthritic hands loosened up and become less painful after three weeks or so of the following nauseating daily treatment. Before going to bed, peel one large strong-smelling onion, cut it in half and put it in a heat-proof glass, pour boiling water over it and lay a saucer over the top. In the morning take out the onion and drink the liquid.

Herbal infusions have been known to help rheumatism and even arthritis in the long run. Agrimony is most popular. For description of infusions see p. 49.

Cold sores   Remember they're very contagious, so don't put your finger back into the ointment after you've applied it, or let your fingers stray round your face. Wash hands thoroughly before and after treating them. Surgical spirit dries them up and is as good as anything.

Encourage your child to acquire healthy diet habits. Reward him or her with fruit and raw vegetables – carrots, celery, etc – instead of sweets, and your child will be on the way to being a healthily slim adult, with better teeth and skin into the bargain.

Fasting   I find a once-a-week fast day keeps my figure and skin in trim. On that day, from the time I get up until I go to bed, I only swallow four tumblers of liquid and no solids. The liquid is the juice-of a lemon and two teaspoonsful of honey in hot water. The lemon is a diuretic, so one spends pennies, and the honey goes straight into the blood stream and prevents one feeling tired. This combination activates my metabolism so the scales weigh on average three pounds lighter next morning.

But this habit of mine may not suit everyone, so, if you have a weight problem it really pays to invest in an annual subscription to *Slimming* magazine which publishes dieting methods to suit all sorts and sizes. They also produce up to date calorie charts – very important this because oddly enough calorie calculations do vary.

Breathing   To reach the top of even the longest flight of stairs without getting out of breath, simply breathe in for three steps and out for three as you go. If your natural breathing rate is either very slow or very fast, adjust the number of steps per breath. A Hollywood star, Clive Brook, told me this after he'd walked up to our seventh-floor flat. He could have gone straight into a Shakespeare soliloquy . . . and he was then in his eightieth year!

For a description of Yoga deep breathing see page 46.

Bruises   You can't stop a bad knock turning multi-coloured because it's caused by the blood bursting from the tiny blood vessels, but rubbing the bruise with an ice-cube will hasten the process. In severe cases some doctors prescribe tablets and creams.

Cider vinegar and honey   Dissolve two teaspoonsful of honey in a little hot water to which are added two teaspoonsful of apple cider vinegar. Half of this should be swallowed first thing in the morning (yes, before that cup of tea), and the rest taken last thing at night. People who have made a habit of taking this concoction regularly never seem to be ailing – and it certainly soothes any tummy upset very quickly.

Swellings   This is a remedy both for a swollen ankle and a swollen, toothaching face. Mix together a handful of flour, one white of egg and three tablespoonsful of vinegar. Put this 'paste' onto some guta perka (green oilskin), place some gauze on the swelling, turn the mixture onto the gauze and bandage firmly. Best left on overnight, but if this is not possible leave for at least two hours. If the symptoms are persistent, go to a doctor or dentist to find out the real cause.

If this sounds far too complicated, a Kaolin poultice works very well. Follow the instructions on the pack or ask your chemist for directions – just be sure to keep *any* poultice well clear of the eyes and nose.

Teeth Superficial stains on teeth will come off with baking powder—first rubbed on dry, then used as a toothpaste. But not too often as it's abrasive and would damage the enamel.

To relieve a toothache before you can get to a dentist, apply a drop or two of oil of cloves, or oil of marjoram to the paining tooth.

Vibro-massagers do not take away surplus fat but they do whip up the circulation and tone muscles. For instance, ski enthusiasts who have only two weeks a year to enjoy the sport, can avoid initial muscle pains if they 'tone' up with a vibro-massager before their holiday.

But go very warily, and only under expert supervision with the facial versions.

Foot care

Each foot has 26 bones jigsawed in neatly with 107 ligaments and 19 muscles and from this cleverly constructed pair, small by comparison to the weight and size they have to carry, we expect a lifetime of service often in return for a minimum of care. That's saying a heck of a lot when you think that in a lifetime the average person walks approximately 65,000 miles (no, I haven't struck a wrong nought).

Bad feet produce the kind of pain one can learn to live with, but at the same time it can etch bitter, aging lines on a face. So we should look after our feet.

Chiropody When in need of foot aid, look for a State Registered Chiropodist ('Ch' pronounced hard, as the word derives from the Greek, not Latin). This brass-plate description is very important because a person has to have had three years' training before they are admitted to the State Register.

Corns The wrong footwear is largely responsible for corns, so getting the right shoes to start with is vital—see *Shoe fittings* below. They form when there's repeated friction over a small area of the foot, and the more elasticity there is in the skin the more resistance it has to friction. Elasticity is reduced when the skin either *lacks* or is *too* greasy, and again when it either lacks moisture or is too sweaty. So, if your feet tend to be dry, massage them generously after having a hot bath, with body lotion or sunflower seed oil. And if they're too greasy or sweaty, wipe them night and morning with a pad of cotton wool soaked in surgical spirit.

Excess hard skin Those pads of hard skin which develop under the sole of our feet are a natural defence mechanism against friction—as protective, especially to dancers, as calloused hands are to a gardener. Unless they hurt they shouldn't be tampered with, and then only by an expert, but the excess hard skin will come off with a touch of pumice stone. Wash your feet, dampen the pumice stone and dip it into a stiff soapy lather, the pointed whipped cream kind, and with circular movements rub it all over the hard pads. Rinse off and when you've dried your feet, massage hand or body lotion or coconut oil well into the skin.

Perspiration Feet tend to perspire profusely, and having them enclosed all the time doesn't help one bit. But it does help to reinforce the effect of regular washing to spray foot deodorant powder not only on the actual feet, but also into the shoes, tights or socks that you're wearing. Apart from curbing any smell, you'll feel more comfortable, and the powder goes a long way to prevent athlete's foot, an unsightly and painful infection easily picked up by going barefoot in swimming baths and hotel rooms, or any public place for that matter.

To improve and soothe sweaty feet put enough potassium permanganate crystals to cover the head of a matchstick (yes, as little as that) into a bowl of comfortably warm water, it'll turn slightly pink. Rest your feet in it for five minutes a day for ten days. The P.P. acts as a tanning agent so abuse this tip and you'll end up with leather-bound feet. And wear wool or wool and cotton socks, if you can find them.

If you tend to have sweaty feet take extra care to cut your toe nails regularly and keep them smoothly filed—perspiration causes the skin to rot, and rotten skin has no resistance to the pressure of a nail that wants to grow inwards.

If you're worried about 'footy' smells despite the use of deodorants, look for boots with cotton linings in the foot section. Men can also get chemically treated socks which neutralise perspiration smells.

Pregnancy When a woman is pregnant, her size obviously increases with her weight. This applies to feet, too, so she may need a larger fitting during those few months. She should keep this in mind and buy new shoes rather than crush her feet painfully into her usual ones.

Sea urchin spines An unpleasant holiday hazard is treading on a sea urchin. Those painful black 'thorns' can be coaxed out by dropping warm candle wax onto your skin. Be careful not to burn yourself by getting the wax too hot. Another method is to keep rubbing a slice of lime over the embedded spikes. The lime juice 'melts' them—lemon doesn't seem to have the same effect.

Shoe fittings Adult fittings don't stay the same; they change roughly every seven years. The size of bones doesn't alter, of course, but joint spaces do, and cause the foot to expand or contract. Remember that feet will lengthen and broaden when stood upon, too. So ask to be measured for your size when you're buying new shoes, and get the assistant to measure your feet *standing up*. He may tell you that manufacturers allow for this, but this allowance can't be an accurate gauge because some feet hardly alter when bearing our full weight, whilst others lengthen as much as half an inch—a pretty important fact when you consider that the difference in a whole shoe size is only one-third of an inch.

It's wiser to buy shoes when your feet are tired and perhaps a bit swollen rather than first thing in the morning when most shoes will feel more comfortable.

The method by which one keeps one's shoes on is very important—any need to grip with the toes should rule out that model.

Never settle for a pair of shoes which need 'breaking in'—the feet will get broken in first.

Tension Though we aren't usually aware of it, we clench our toes in times of tension, just as we clench our fists. It throws out the balance and fit of our shoes, and encourages that fatal corn-producing friction.

Yoga

Hatha Yoga (one of several branches of Yoga) is the oldest physical culture system in the world; it combines exercising and breathing with a way of thinking. You don't have to delve into any deeper meanings to benefit from it, though. Simply doing a few exercises which suit you as an individual combined with the Yoga method of breathing can help relax nerves, encourage sleep and even control weight to a certain extent.

There is no 'right' age for taking up Yoga—young and old of different temperaments and mentalities can adapt Yoga to their own varied physical and spiritual needs. You should have some lessons from a Yoga teacher to begin with. If you try to learn from books you may not get the right ideas and could practise the asanas (exercises) wrongly. Nowadays most health clubs and centres either teach Yoga or can give you the address of a teacher. Your local authority may run evening classes.

What I can do here is to describe the Yoga method of deep breathing, which is very relaxing and refreshing.

The complete Yoga breath fills us with revitalising air while pushing out all the stale stuff. (Our usual breathing is very shallow and when we're told to breathe deeply we tend to push out our chests, lift our shoulders and achieve very little.) So...with mouth closed, very slowly inhale through your nostrils during a slow count of six. Imagine that your breath starts way down in your feet, creeps slowly up your legs, and reaches your tummy, so that when it fills your tummy this should automatically swell *out* (usually at this stage we're pulling it in). Let the air keep travelling up past your ribs until finally it fills up your lungs — only now should your chest swell up. You'll probably find you haven't the breath to last the trip.

Hold that breath now for the count of four, then gradually reverse the process, breathing out through the nostrils for a count of six. As the air goes out past your tummy let it sink in as it empties.

Although you may find at first that you haven't enough breath for the whole trip, you'll be surprised how quickly you'll increase your breathing power with steady practice. It's the slow, rhythmical rate which helps to calm down your whole system and relax you.

One is often told when learning to breathe deeply to 'make your mind a blank'. This is easier said than done, so it may help to try, as I do, to think of a spot in the middle of your forehead. Concentrating on this spot, making it any colour, texture or size, does sweep all daily worries from one's mind and by then the rhythmical breathing takes over and helps you to relax.

Vitamins and minerals

Vitamins

Vitamins regulate the building and repair of the body, and control the chemical reactions that take place in the body cells.

A sensible, varied diet will provide all the necessary vitamins and minerals when a body is in good working order, but if you feel you need an added boost the following list will give you a superficial idea of which ones do what for us.

Vitamins are essential to our health in daily quantities of only a few milligrammes per day.

Vitamin A

Encourages good eyesight, increases the melanin in our skin, so protects against sunburn and strengthens us against infections.

Sources of vitamin A: liver, cod liver oil, butter, cheese, milk, carrots and tomatoes.

Lack of vitamin A causes: eye inflammations, dry itchy skin, loss of hair, painful swelling of the arms and leg bones.

Too much vitamin A causes: loss of appetite, loss of hair, pains in arm and leg bones.

Vitamin B1 (thiamine)

Nourishes nerve cells; stimulates the appetite, helps to break down carbohydrates.

Sources of vitamin B1: yeast, cereals, and wheat germ.

Lack of vitamin B1 (and all vitamin B groups) causes: beri-beri — an oriental disease which produces nerve and brain damage, swelling of hands and legs.

You can't take too much B1.

Vitamin B2 (riboflavin)

Aids general growth; helps to ventilate cells. Healthy hair; enlivens the brain.

Sources of vitamin B2: liver, kidney, milk, meat extracts, green vegetables galore, mushrooms.

Lack of vitamin B2 causes: splits at the corners of the mouth, dermatitis, itching and burning of eyes and tongue.

You can't take too much B2.

Vitamin B12 (cyanocobalamin)

Increases the production of red blood corpuscles; boosts energy. Speeds production of bile salts thus reducing level of cholesterol in the blood — slows down nerve cell degeneration.

Sources of vitamin B12: liver, kidney, other red meats, milk, cheese and eggs, so if you are a Vegan, the strictest vegetarian, you *must* take B12 supplements.

Lack of vitamin B12 causes: anaemia, pernicious anaemia.

You can't take too much B12.

Vitamin C (ascorbic acid)

Helps to form and maintain cartilage and tissues between the cells. Vitalises the blood stream and helps build up walls of blood vessels.

Sources of vitamin C: citrus fruits, currants, berries, melons, lettuce, green peppers, raw cabbage.

Lack of vitamin C causes: scurvy, spongy bleeding gums, loosening teeth; delays the healing of wounds, haemorrhages.

Too much vitamin C causes: diarrhoea, kidney stones.

Vitamin D

The 'sunshine' vitamin — encourages the absorption of both calcium and phosphorus into the body, which we need to strengthen our bones. Particularly important for pregnant women. Helps muscles to stay pliable; important for sound teeth.

Sources of vitamin D: ultraviolet light on the skin from the sun; animal fats (animals and birds get what they need from licking their fur and feathers). Tuna, sardines, cod liver oil, herring, tinned salmon, margarine, eggs and butter.

Lack of vitamin D causes: rickets in children and another version of the same thing in adults — softening of the bone through lack of calcium.

Too much vitamin D causes: calcification (hardening) of non-bony tissues, including lungs and kidney. Loss of appetite and sickness.

Vitamin E

Improves glandular health and increases the production of vital hormones so it activates the reproductive organs in both males and females. Recent studies in the States have led researchers to believe that this vitamin keeps our 'machinery' working in top form.

Sources of vitamin E: vegetable fats made from corn, soya beans, peanut, coconut and cotton seed are the richest sources.

Lack of vitamin E causes: sterility in male rats, and although the females can conceive normally, the offspring die in the womb. What effect its lack has in men and women hasn't been determined yet because almost every foodstuff we use contains vitamin E, but it is thought to begin with sterility, loss of hair and poor blood circulation.

You can't take too much vitamin E.

Vitamin K

Keeps the blood-clotting process on an even keel.

Sources of vitamin K: dark green vegetables, especially kale, spinach and nettles.

Lack of vitamin K causes: haemorrhaging.

You can't take too much vitamin K.

Minerals

Minerals are important for body building, particularly the skeleton and the blood. But as with vitamins a good varied diet provides all we need as a rule.

Calcium and phosphorus

Necessary for good bone and teeth formation, help the heart muscles and nerves to work well.

Sources: milk, cheese, egg yolk, asparagus, cauliflower, cabbage, beans and lentils. (Pregnant women should increase their intake of calcium.)

Lack of calcium causes: fragile bones and teeth.

Fluorine

In small quantities it helps to develop and strengthen the teeth. Most effective during pregnancy for the benefit of the unborn child. In large quantities it is poisonous and causes kidney trouble.

Source: water.

Iodine

Produces thyroid hormone.

Source: iodised salt, seaweed.

Lack of iodine causes: goitre swelling, supersensitivity to the cold, dry skin, anaemia, general slowing down of reaction, falling hair.

Iron

Enriches the blood and nourishes the cells.

Sources: spinach, liver, heart, kidney, oysters, fish, nuts, molasses, oatmeal.

Lack of iron causes: listlessness, lack of energy, vague pains everywhere, anaemia.

Overdose of iron causes: liver damage, patchy skin pigmentation, eventually diabetes.

Magnesium

Seventy per cent magnesium combined with calcium and phosphorus make up bone. Plays an important part in cell metabolism.

Sources: nuts, soya beans, cocoa.

Lack of magnesium causes: dizziness, depression.

Overdose of magnesium causes: excessive sleepiness.

Potassium

Activates muscles and adjusts water retention.

Sources: chicken, meat, green vegetables and fruit.

Lack of potassium causes: heart trouble.

Overdose of potassium causes: slow pumping of heart muscle, weakness in limbs, muddle-headedness.

Sodium

Curbs fluid loss and is active in cell metabolism.

Sources: salt, bread, cheese, carrots, celery, nuts, oysters.

Lack of sodium causes: muscle cramps, headaches, sickness and diarrhoea.

Herbs

I expect you all use herbs for cooking. But did you know it was the Romans, during the four hundred years they were in Britain, who first sowed the seeds of parsley, chives, onion, fennel, rosemary, borage, sage, and so on?

The use of herbs in medicines goes back even further — there are records of herbal medicines in Ancient Egypt. There is no doubt that they have healing powers: they may take a little time to work, but they have the advantage of producing no bad side effects.

Today cosmetic manufacturers all over the world are well aware of the beautifying and health giving effects of herbs on skin and hair, and they've been used as firm and trusted friends of lovelies through the ages.

The basic methods of extracting the active qualities from herbs are infusions and decoctions.

Infusions, such as tisanes, are made by pouring boiling water over the herb, just like tea — usually one teaspoonful of herbs to a teacupful of water. They should be left to stand a little longer than tea before being drunk.

Decoctions are made by pouring a pint of water on roots, barks and wood, then boiling them until the liquid has been reduced by about one-third.

Cures for temperatures and colds should be drunk piping hot, but it doesn't matter whether the others are taken hot or cold.

To dry herbs   Pick herbs on a dry day but before the sun's too hot. Take care not to damage the leaves and don't keep the discoloured ones. You can 'instant-dry' herbs on a baking sheet in a very low oven — keep a watch on them and turn them carefully until they're brittle. But the old-fashioned way is to dry them on white lining paper, laid in a cardboard box kept in a warm place, under the bed for instance, in an airing cupboard or the warming drawer of the cooker. Turn them each day until they get brittle, probably a week or so — they should then be bone dry. But to make sure, keep them in a screw-topped glass jar for a day or two — if any moisture shows on the glass, lay them out to dry for a few more days.

Once dried, store herbs in air-tight glass jars and keep them well away from the light. They'll keep their scent better if you pack them whole and only crumble them when you need them.

Herbal tisanes (a few of many)

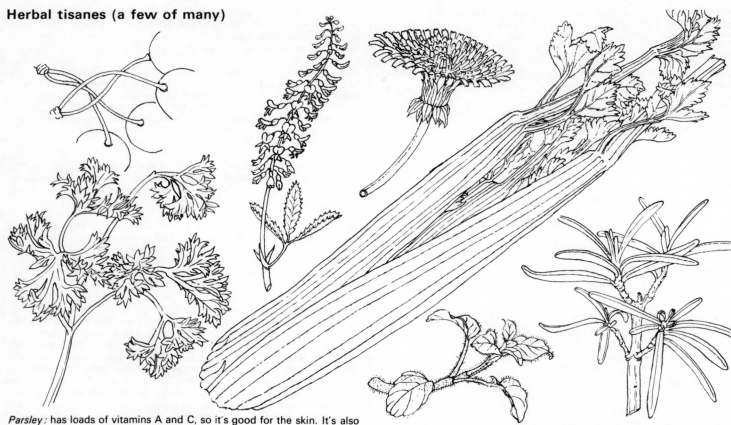

Parsley: has loads of vitamins A and C, so it's good for the skin. It's also a diuretic, so helps when on a diet.

Dandelion tea: is a gentle laxative—is useful in cases of ensuing kidney troubles, diabetes, skin diseases and irritated female organs.

Celery tea: soothes rheumatic pains.

Marjoram: helps to sweat out the start of a cold.

Cherry stalk tea: relieves bronchial sufferers and helps fight anaemia.

Melilot tea: valuable as an anti-coagulant which helps to keep a pure blood steam.

Rosemary: encourages sleep—delicious when laced with a little honey. Can also be inhaled to destuff a blocked nose. Adds strength and vitality to thin, dull hair.

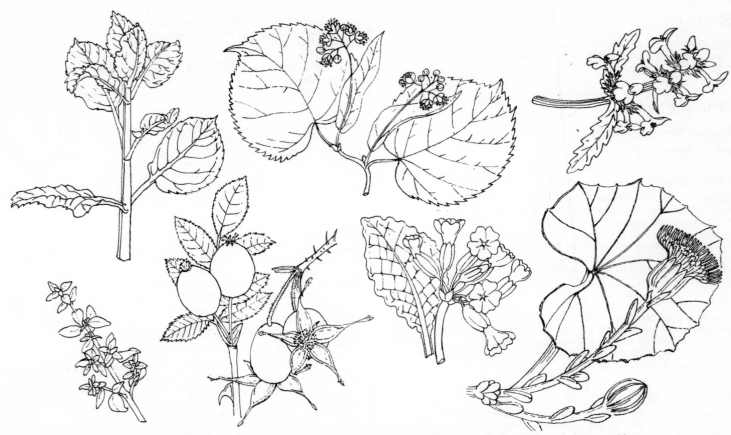

Camomile tea, cowslip flowers: soothe nerves and encourage sleep.

Wood betony tea: soothes nervous headaches, rheumatism and dyspepsia. Helps skin troubles.

Rose hip tea: rich in vitamin C.

Thyme: relieves coughs and sinus ailments.

Coltsfoot: helps to relieve catarrh and chest troubles.

Lime blossom tea: fights insomnia, nervous indigestion and tiredness. Also helps clear catarrh after a cold.

Mint tea: helps digestion; anti-nausea and helps prevent flatulence. Chew some raw mint leaves when you're on a diet and those hunger pangs won't hurt half as much.

Beauty

In this section I'm dealing with the beauty side of health and beauty — how to care for your body, eyes, hair, hands and skin, together with some information on make-up and plastic surgery.

Body care

Caring for your back

See the **Health** section, p. 41.

Circulation

Cellulitis This is a circulatory disturbance which bothers a lot of women, causing that lumpy, sometimes painful 'orange peel' look on the skin, usually concentrated around the thighs and upper arms. It is thought to be caused by our hormonal mechanism; contributing factors may be lack of exercise, over-eating and even too much stress. It should be tackled at the initial stages with massage using special creams, diet, and specific leg exercises. Slimming, health and beauty clubs are now able to give help on the subject.

Crossing your legs can curb circulation and could encourage varicose veins. To give a free flow to the blood, as well as the longest line possible to your legs, stretch one slightly sideways, then cross the other leg over it and lay it parallel to the first so that one foot rests just above the ankle of the other. It's comfortable, too.

Diet

There isn't really such a thing as middle-aged spread. Usually people grow fatter as they grow older simply because they take less exercise while eating as much as (or more than) they always did. Glandular malfunction, blamed so often by fatties, is relatively rare; the most overworked gland ... is the *mouth*.

If you find it difficult to stick to a diet, simply halve the quantity of everything you usually eat. Unless you're a glutton, this step in the right direction should show results after a week or so, and the incentive will probably encourage you to halve that half quantity again. Chew very slowly and don't eat a heavy meal in the evening when your metabolism is slowing down for the night.

I find fasting helps keep me in good trim — see page 42 under general health hints.

Isometrics

These are exercises which strengthen and tone the body and help turn the fat into muscle; they can be done surreptitiously throughout the day. They work by putting one set of muscles to work against another or against an immovable object. For example, when you're standing in a queue, pull in your tummy and push your knees back to tighten the inner thigh muscles. When you're sitting in a car or at dinner, pull in your tummy muscles and clench your thigh muscles against the seat or chair.

Perspiration

There are two types of sweat gland — the eccrine and the apocrine. The eccrine glands control our body temperature so that when we get hot they overflow with a mildly salt liquid and cool us off. This liquid doesn't smell at all. The unpleasant smell of perspiration comes from the apocrine glands which exude a creamy sweat made up of fatty acids, urea and ammonia as well as salt and water. This solution decomposes the minute bacteria which we all have on our skin, and it's this process which causes that characteristic smell. It's worse, of course, in the airless and enclosed areas of our body such as armpits.

Lots of factors influence our sweating — the weather, different types of clothing, our emotions and our health. So although scrupulous cleanliness and regular washing is a must, it isn't always the complete answer. The bacteria have got to be killed or prevented from growing, and this is where deodorants and anti-perspirants come in.

Deodorants reduce the bacteria count, and daily use is usually enough to stop any unpleasant smell for twenty-four hours.

Anti-perspirants actually reduce perspiration. They contain aluminium salts which work on the glands to stop the wetness, and contain a bactericide so that they act as a deodorant as well. No two brands of anti-perspirant are identical, and people's reactions vary too, which means that we've just got to find the particular brand which suits us best. But the ones used on a clean, hair-free body are likely to be the most effective.

Here's how to get the best use from your deodorant or anti-perspirant:

Aerosol anti-perspirants can be shared hygienically by all the family because, unlike the roll-on types, the applicator doesn't touch the skin.

After shaving   It's a good idea to wait an hour or so before using an anti-perspirant, though as products are always being improved this is becoming less of a problem.

Allergies are usually caused by the perfume and not the basic properties of an anti-perspirant, so if this is your problem just ask for an unscented version.

Feet perspire more heavily on some people than others, but regular washing is essential, of course, and there are deodorant powders and sprays on the market—spray them in your shoes and stockings, as well as your feet. You can also buy chemically treated socks which neutralise perspiration smells (see also page 45).

Scent
Scent or eau de toilette lingers longer if applied to the warmest parts of the body which are the pulse spots—inside bend of your elbows, inner wrists, base of throat or behind the knees, but also wherever you, as an individual 'hot up' most: perhaps between your breasts; back of your neck etc.

Tummy muscles
Here are two good exercises for a flat, firm, flab-free tummy.

1   Provided you haven't got back trouble, do this exercise ten times or so daily. Lie flat on the floor, raise your legs keeping them straight, and aim to form a right-angle with your body. Don't worry if you can't make this at first. Then, very slowly, lower your legs to the ground, still keeping them straight and without lifting your head. The reverse version helps a

lot, too: keep your legs straight and glued to the floor (perhaps anchored under a heavy piece of furniture) while you raise your head, shoulders and trunk up and reach for your toes with your finger tips. You'll probably ache next day but in ten days you should start to notice the difference.

2   You can form a natural girdle with your muscles—unless you've had a serious operation and your doctor advises against it. Just tuck in your tail and pull your tummy in to meet it. Keep breathing. Make a habit of doing this whether you're standing, sitting or even lying down, and you'll soon have a flatter tummy to show for your effort.

You and your skin

A beautiful, healthy skin is to make-up what a smooth canvas is to painting and there's no doubt that sensible and regular skin care does reduce blemishes and delay the effects of aging.

Our skin is divided into two main layers: the epidermis, or cuticle, and the dermis, or corium, which are in turn subdivided.

The epidermis is made up of cells which dry, die, and are continually being renewed, whilst in the dermis and its sub-divisions lie the blood vessels, the hair follicles, the nerve ends, the muscles and the sebaceous glands— it's when the sebum flows too freely from these glands, blocking the pores, that we get acne. The cells of the epidermis can't be fed, but the dermis does absorb a certain amount of nourishment. This has been proved beyond a shadow of a doubt because, after the use of cortisone and other steroid ointments over too long a period, a patient has to be given injections to counteract their action on the adrenalin glands.

There are various types of skin, and manufacturers go to great pains to produce the skin care and make-up products suitable for them, so take care to buy the right ones for your particular complexion. If you don't, you'll be doing yourself and the makers a disservice. And never be snooty about the lower-priced ranges of make-up; they are excellent and often packed in small containers, so they're just the thing to experiment with.

Skin types

Normal skin   This has neither enlarged pores nor flaky, dry patches; it's smooth all over and doesn't turn make-up orangey. The odd eruption might occur around menstruation time when the hormone content of the body alters and causes the sebaceous glands to be overactive.

Cleanse with a light cleansing cream or milk. Wash afterwards if you wish with soap and tepid water—this will never harm a normal skin. Tone with a freshener—during the menstruation period you might need a light astringent to counteract the overflow of sebum from the sebaceous glands. Then apply a moisturising cream; always use one under your make-up, particularly around the eye area and on the neck.

Greasy skin   This type of skin has a coarse texture with open pores. It's prone to spots, turns make-up orangey and goes shiny very quickly. The oily build-up has got to be removed continually. You can do this from the inside by cutting down on fried, spicy food and chocolates, whilst eating lots of raw vegetables, salads and fruits.

For external care, use a medicated cleanser, then wash with a liquid medicated soap and tepid water. The pores must be kept unclogged and coaxed to close with cotton wool pads soaked with astringent. A face mask twice a week will help to keep the pores oil-free. Even a greasy skin needs a moisturiser to encourage those outer cells to soften and slough off as well as to protect the skin, but only a light film is needed before applying make-up.

Dry skin   This type has dry, flaky patches, looks dull and starts showing fine lines at a very early age. Spots are very rare. Cold weather makes it red and sore.

It needs a rich, creamy or liquifying cleansing cream. No soap and water, and only tone with mineral water on a pad of cotton wool or a half-and-half mixture of witch hazel and rosewater. Wear a rich moisturiser or even a light nourishing cream under your make-up, and a thicker, though never tacky, nourishing cream at night. I've taken to adding the contents of either a wheatgerm capsule or liquid vitamin E oil to any night cream. Find a special eye cream which suits you, that is, one that doesn't cause your eyelids to puff up overnight and pat a little on lightly for both day and night wear. Dry skin must be given extra care from one's teens, or it will age very early on in life.

Combination skin There are very many of these around. A combination skin consists of a greasy panel from forehead down to the chin, with all the symptoms of a dry skin on the cheeks and the outer edges of the face and neck.

This complexion naturally has to be treated in separate sections as for both dry and greasy skins. If done cleverly and with perseverance, a balance can be achieved. In other words, use face packs and astringents down the oily strip while keeping the cheeks and outer edges moisturised and nourished and toned with a freshener instead of astringent and so on throughout. The initial outlay in beauty products is twice as much, but of course they will last twice as long!

Skin care

In this section I shall be dealing with different aspects of skin care—facial hair, general hints, masks, necks and chins, skin care on holiday, and spots.

Spots

Basically, spots are blocked pores which erupt and overflow, and they can be caused by lots of things, from eating too much spicy or greasy food, a malfunctioning metabolism, to simple dirt—putting on make-up with grubby fingers, for example, and using unwashed brushes and other make-up 'tools'.

Cleanliness Absolutely scrupulous cleanliness is a must, inside as well as out. A tumblerful of hot water sipped last thing every single night and very first thing in the morning tastes horrible—but it does clean the skin.

General hints

Broken veins are easier to prevent than to get rid of. They are caused by too-hot as well as too-cold water, so avoid both at all costs. Cold winds can cause them, too, so protect your skin with moisturiser and a base when facing wicked weather conditions.

Cool it! When the weather's too hot for comfort, tepid baths or showers keep you cooler than cold water which closes the pores and raises the body heat.

Freckles Freckles are small areas where the pigment changes quicker in certain areas of the skin when exposed to sunlight than in the surrounding areas. They show up more in the summer than in winter. Nothing can really get rid of these marks but they'll fade a little if you dip a stubby make-up brush into lemon juice and brush the freckled area—leave it on for fifteen minutes or more, then wash off with soapy warm water.

An old wives' tale worth trying is to put a daily smear of castor oil onto freckled hands and massage it right in until it disappears. I don't quite see how it can, but, who knows, it might work in the long run.

Here are two more tips for removing them just for the record—I've never seen them work myself, although two ex-freckled friends swear they do!

Cover fresh elderberries with cold distilled water and stand overnight. Strain and wash your face with the liquid. Continue daily until the freckles vanish.

Mix together about a teaspoonful of freshly grated horseradish to a tablespoonful of milk. Leave to stand before applying to the face daily.

A freshener An excellent mild skin freshener you can make yourself is a half-and-half mixture of witch hazel and rosewater.

Rough skin If your arms and thighs are rough and blotchy, your circulation needs a boost. Get a loofah, and when you're in a hot bath give yourself a thorough rub down with it. Dry with a rough towel, then smooth in body lotion. With daily treatment you'll soon notice the improvement.

If your heels, knees and elbows are very rough, spread sunflower seed oil over them *before* stepping into a hot bath, then work it in while you're soaking. Afterwards wash with soap as usual.

Oatmeal will soften water if you tie a few handfuls up in some muslin and leave this in the bath while the water's running.

Scorch marks If you've played with fire during the winter and have leftover scorch marks on your legs, this 'mask' helps to fade them if used daily for a week – the juice of a lemon, the white of an egg (more of both if needed), mixed to a paste with carbonate of magnesium. Spread this over the marks, allow to harden, then soak off with tepid water. If your skin has become wafer thin and flaky put on a film of moisture cream before applying the mask. Burn Ointment made by Alo Cosmetics will also help to fade scorch marks.

Vitamin E According to Dr Alloys Tappel, American food researcher and professor of the University of California, Vitamin E can delay the aging process of the body cells. When eaten in the form of wheatgerm sprinkled over food it is nerve-nourishing, energy-giving and supposedly increases both sexiness and fertility. Used on one's skin it helps to heal and eradicate scars and certainly it softens lines too. I buy the capsules by the gross, swallow a few daily and puncture a few more with an ever ready safety pin, and add the contents to my night cream. And I add half a teaspoonful of Vitamin E oil to my moisture cream, mix well and put a film of this mixture on under my foundation. A very good tip this if you have extra dry skin.

Wrinkles To soften expression lines, particularly those running from nostrils to mouth and between the eyebrows; with no make-up on, cream or oil them, then between thumb and forefinger pinch them *across* the way they run.

A home-made but effective party wrinkle smoother (commercial ones which could overstretch the skin are no longer available) is to smear raw egg white on the tell-tale lines, and allow to dry before applying make-up.

Masks

Masks absorb oil and grime, help coax out blackheads, slough off dead skin, stimulate the circulation and temporarily tighten pores. When you buy a mask make sure it's the type made specially for your kind of skin. In all cases masks should be spread on evenly, avoiding the eyes and the mouth, and kept on without changing your facial expression until they have dried – approximately 10–15 minutes, then usually washed off with plenty of tepid water.

Clay masks harden, clay-like, and do an excellent job on a greasy skin because they absorb the oil. As the mask dries it shrinks and lifts out all the impurities from the pores.

My own home-made mask Take a half-and-half mixture of kaolin and magnesium carbonate and mix into a paste with calamine lotion. Spread it on thickly and allow to set. Slough off with tepid water. Ease off with cotton wool soaked in water so as not to drag the skin.

Moisturising masks cleanse as they add moisture. They're creamy and just right for normal-to-dry skins. You can use them up to twice a week.

A home-made mask in this category is made by mashing enough oatmeal and grated cucumber together to give a moist consistency which clings to the skin. Spread it on thickly and leave for ten minutes – then massage it off with tepid water.

Peel-off masks If applied correctly and left to dry completely, these should peel off in a single transparent sheet, bringing with it the impurities from the pores and a few dead cells into the bargain. Great sloughers and smoothers, but unless you're a grease spot, don't use more than once a week.

Neck and chin care

A youthful skin includes a nice smooth chin and neck, so follow these tips for complete skin beauty.

Crepy necks can be improved or even prevented. Each night, cream the neck either with a special neck cream or a nourishing cream – even that old stand-by sunflower seed oil will do. Massage it well into the surface with small, firm, circular movements until the boosted circulation has made the neck pink and a lot of cream is absorbed. Now fluff on some baby powder and go to bed. In the morning repeat the creaming session with less cream, and don't make the neck too pink this time. Then fluff on lots of baby powder and this time wipe away any excess with a tissue so that clothes don't get messed up. After the first few times the skin will already look and feel smoother. It won't hurt to nourish the neck during the day too – wipe off excess hand cream onto your neck, it'll lap it up.

A double, treble chin will shrink if, having creamed it well, you tuck in your neck as 'ugly-ly' as possible. Then with thumbs and forefingers, pinch and *push* chunks of the flesh – careful not to 'pull' or you'll bruise the skin.

To exercise neck and chin muscles say 'Q' then 'E' very exaggeratedly, as many times as you can every day. Do it in front of a looking glass to start with – you may look funny, but you'll see the pulling effect it has.

To smooth the jawline and shrink those 'squirrel pouches': first remove make-up and cream the skin. Then point hands downwards, keeping fore-fingers very straight, and stroke them firmly but smoothly along the jawline, starting from the centre of the chin and working to the base of the ears. Repeat as many times as possible. Then, between thumb and forefinger, push the skin firmly up along and into the jawline. *Never* try this or any other skin 'kneading' without first taking off make-up and creaming the skin.

Skin care on holiday

Stings   If you're stung by a jelly fish or 'man of war', rub handfuls of wet sand firmly over the area – the pain subsides quite quickly and so do the 'whiplash' marks. This is no old wives' tale – time and again it has worked miraculously. It was taught me by a wise old fisherman who always stood barelegged in the water.

Sunburn can be soothed and helped to be cured by wearing long-sleeved cotton shirts and trousers soaked in water – and keeping them wet. Useful in the case of active children – this is hydrotherapy in action.

Tanning   When a skin tans easily this is due to the quantity of melanin in the skin's cell metabolism. When this is exposed to the sun it alters the pigmentation so as to protect it from the ultraviolet rays. So long as one continues to encourage this process with sun tanning lotions and nourishes the skin extra generously after tanning sessions – also keeping up a regular skin care routine – there will be no lasting harmful effects, because the dried surface cells will just slough off with the fading tan.

That 'mottled' look you get when suntan is wearing off is just the top layer of skin coming away in patches. Help it on its way with a good scrub down with a loofah when you're in the bath. You'll be a shade lighter, but it'll be an even colour again. Use body lotion or cream after you've dried yourself. If you've run out of lotion, a cotton wool pad soaked with milk is a good alternative.

Here's a tanning lotion you can make yourself – but it's for easy tanners only: two-thirds of olive oil to one-third brown vinegar, shaken up well together.

To keep pores clear keep a very clean flannel especially for this purpose. Once a week – having removed your make-up – dip the flannel in hot water, wring it out and press it against your face and neck. Do this a few times, then sloosh the skin with tepid to cold water, and apply a face mask. Always ask for the kind of mask to suit your own type of complexion – see *Masks* on page 56.

To speed a spot to a head   Wring out a pad of clean cotton wool in hot water and press it gently on the spot so that the skin softens, the pores open and the blood comes to the surface. Now pat dry and apply a paste made of glycerine and Epsom salts. Leave on overnight. Next morning, wipe the skin clean with another pad of cotton wool soaked in hot water, then wrap round your two forefingers a tissue and gently press round the spot with your finger pads – never be tempted to use your nails. If the spot won't burst, leave it, and just wipe over with a touch of surgical spirit. Wear a film of flesh-coloured anti-acne cream during the day. This will keep working on the spot and will blend in with your make-up at the same time. In the evening repeat the whole process. When the spot has con-veniently come to a head a little pressure should get rid of it. Dab with surgical spirit to prevent re-infection. It is still a good idea to wear a touch of that special cream until the trace has completely disappeared.

Spotty complexions on both boys and girls can benefit from this method and a weekly cleanse with an old-fashioned creamy mask works wonders.

'Spring-cleaning'   This is a super 'from the inside' skin cleaner, and doesn't taste too bad. Mix a heaped teaspoonful of powdered flowers of sulphur with the same amount of runny honey, and take nightly for ten days. But nothing beats a glass of hot water sipped regularly last thing at night and first thing in the morning.

Facial hair

Bleaching   Here's a home-made bleach for facial hair – effective if the growth isn't too heavy: two drops ammonia, one dessertspoonful 20 volume peroxide, mixed to a paste with Kaolin. Spread onto the hair – leave on for ten minutes or so – rinse off well.

An alternative home-made bleach is to mix two tablespoonful of 20 volume peroxide with five or six drops of ammonia and add enough mild soap-flakes to make a paste. Apply it immediately and leave on for ten minutes. Rinse off well. If the results aren't light enough or there's a reddish tint to the hair mix the same paste in a day or so and start again.

Depilatories   Make sure they're specifically for *facial* hair. And be careful you're not allergic to any particular one. You should do a patch test by rubbing a little of the depilatory cream into the skin on the inside bend of your elbow, behind your ear, or even behind your knee, and leave it on for twenty-four hours. If there's any reaction whatsoever, try another make.

Electrolysis   This is the only permanent method of removing hair, but its success depends on the skill of the operator.

Plucking   This *can* cause splitting of the roots so that several hairs grow in little clumps from each new root.

Shaving   *Don't.* Anyway, it's depressing for a woman to have to.

Waxing   There are two schools of thought on this. Some say it will weaken the growth, others say just the opposite. It certainly removes the down as well as the coarse hair, so when this grows through again it does appear darker and more noticeable. However, all the regrowth is actually fine and tapered, unlike the stubbly one on a shaved surface.

Hair beauty

Bleaching

If you have a permanent wave on top of a bleach, and/or vice versa, it does dry out the hair and encourage it to split. Don't let anyone kid you this isn't so! Rather than giving yourself the problems of an overall bleach, which will need continual re-touching and unless you use lashings of con-ditioner will make your hair brittle, light streaks can give a very flattering lift to dark hair. To do it yourself: brush your hair, then push it into a plastic bag and tie a string round your head down over it on the hair line to keep it in place. Now, with a small, sharp crochet hook, dig through the plastic and fish out a few (very few) strands of hair. Go over your whole head pulling out these minute tufts – you'll look a fright, but the ends should justify the means! That done, plaster over the tufts and the plastic cap with the bleach, and wait. (The instructions on the bleach bottle will tell you how long – careful not to overdo it.) When your time's up, rinse off the bleach, take off the plastic bag, and after a shampoo and set your hair should look sunkissed and seductive!

Conditioners

Hair which is in good condition under the microscope looks like the scales of a fish – each one overlapping the next, lying flat and shiny over the centre stem. Hair in bad condition has damaged scales. Conditioners come in two categories. There are those which smooth down the damaged scales, but only superficially so that they appear temporarily glossy and a comb can run effortlessly through the hair—these are the ones which are put on after the shampoo and left on when the hair is set. The other sort are re-conditioners, which lift the scales so as to reach and nourish the marrow of the hair as well as glossing down the scales; these are the products which are put on after the shampoo but only left on for a few minutes to do the 'feeding', then rinsed off before setting the hair. If your hair is very dry massage in and comb through one of these re-conditioners before going to bed—sleep in a bath cap. Next morning wash and set your hair, or tie on a scarf and skulk to the hairdresser. You'll notice the improvement in the condition of your hair.

Home-made re-conditioners   This is excellent for damaged and dry hair. Mix one whole raw egg, plus one extra yolk, with a generous tot of rum. Massage this mixture well into the hair and scalp and leave on as long as possible. I have combed it through on holiday and gone for a long walk along a sun-soaked beach—yes, the alcoholic fumes did get me a few weird looks! Then rinse out, with cool water at first, or you'll end up with a rum omelette—and set as usual.

Another home-made conditioner, especially convenient when funds are low, is to blend an egg yolk with a tablespoonful of olive oil. After shampooing massage the mixture into the hair, wrap a warm towel round the head and leave for five minutes. Heat up the towel once or twice. Finally rinse off thoroughly with warm (not hot) water.

Oils   Olive and other vegetable oils nourish hair well but will lift the colour on bleached or tinted tresses. The exception is coconut oil. Asians use this as a regular beauty treatment to keep their hair gloriously thick and shiny, but I've found it invaluable to re-condition tired, split hair. Pour coconut oil generously over the hair, massage it well in and comb through so that every strand gets coated. Then encourage the oil to soak in by any of the following methods: sit or walk in the sun; or wear a plastic bag over the head and wrap a towel round turban-wise on top of it; or steam the oil in by wringing out a towel in very hot water and wrapping round the head again turban-wise. Repeat as soon as the towel has cooled even slightly. After this treatment, pour some shampoo straight onto the hair, *then* add the water so the oil comes out more easily. Rinse well, add a cream conditioner so as to comb it easily, rinse off and set.

Vinegar   If you're out of a conditioner a few tablespoonsful of vinegar in the final rinse will give hair a shine and ease the comb through it.

Beer   A can of beer poured over hair after the final rinse, then set, gives hair more body and the smell wears off as it dries.

Cutting

Healthy hair grows at the rate of half an inch a month. The warmth makes hair grow faster so it usually grows more quickly in the summer.

I won't swear to this, but a lot of people do. Cut hair when there's a new moon, and it will grow longer; cut it when the moon wanes and it will grow thicker. It's for sure, though, that to club cut even the finest hair will make it feel and look thicker.

Dry hair

Always use a bristle brush for dry hair—the ends are less likely to split. And see **Conditioners** above.

Greasy hair

The cause of greasy hair is over-active sebaceous glands. Anything which stimulates the scalp—shampooing, brushing, tugging roughly with a comb, scratching the scalp with a comb, will increase the problem by encouraging these glands to produce more grease. So go gently with it, and use a comb rather than a brush. It's wiser to use a bone comb, second best are vulcanite and I'd bypass the steel ones.

Diet   You can treat greasy hair from the inside, too, with lots of fresh fruit and raw vegetables—salads, carrots, celery, lettuce, tomatoes and so on. Avoid fried or spicy foods.

To remove grease from long hair (or even straighten it) this tip is old-fashioned but very effective. Lay your tresses on the ironing board and then put brown wrapping paper on them, shiny side up, and iron over it. For heaven's sake, never iron your hair without the protection of the paper.

Here's a quick party pick-me-up. Make lots of partings, then with cotton wool soaked in eau de cologne, wipe along the roots. Don't rub hard or you'll get those sebaceous glands overflowing faster. Baby powder dusted on and then brushed out will help extra-greasy hair. And Gem Instant Shampoo puffs on and brushes out.

Shampooing   Shampoo greasy hair *less* often rather than more. Put the shampoo on without dampening the hair first, then add water gradually — the grease will come off more easily. Go very gently over the scalp while shampooing.

Pony tails

If you can't find those covered bands — tie your hair back with a pipe cleaner rather than an elastic band — it's kinder to your hair.

A rinse for blonde hair

To make your blonde hair shine and bring out every golden glint, try this as a final rinse. Make an infusion of strong camomile tea: pour boiling water over two teaspoonsful of camomile and leave to stand for ten minutes. (Camomile is obtainable from most health stores.)

Setting your hair

Beer's a good stand-in for setting lotion — the smell will go as soon as you brush out your hair.

Fine, breakable hair can be protected by covering your non-heated rollers with bits of foam rubber (the thinnest sheets you can buy), tucking them in at the ends with a touch of glue. Then they'll be very kind to the hair.

Heated rollers won't dry out your hair — even if you don't add conditioner — if you wrap a layer of soft loo paper round each one before warming and using them. The 'wrapping' should last through three or four sets without having to be renewed.

When setting your hair on heated rollers, instead of spraying lacquer on after you've done your hair, which can give a 'solid' overall effect, puff a little onto each tuft just before you roll it on. Then, when you brush your hair out, the set will stay in firmly but the hair will still 'move' naturally.

Putting in rollers so that the results look professional: the secret is to 'lift' the hair at the roots. Comb the section of hair at the roots. Comb the section of hair, making it no wider than the roller is long, then pull it in the opposite direction to the way it grows, and keeping it taut all the time, put in the roller so it ends up lying as near the base of that section as possible.

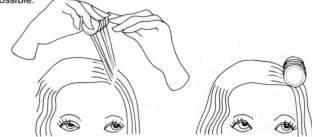

Your set will last longer if you give your hair time to cool off when you come out of the dryer before removing rollers and brushing out.

To straighten hair

Comb through the perm lotion of your home-perm set. Be careful not to pull at all hard on the hair while it's soaked in this lotion, as it's extremely fragile at this stage. Then shampoo off thoroughly. Be extra generous with conditioner afterwards to revitalise your hair, and set on very large rollers.

Washing

If you have to wash your hair every two or three days you'll be stripping it of its natural oils, so use a herbal shampoo, they are the mildest ones of all, and one shampoo should be plenty.

For shampooing greasy hair, see under **Greasy hair,** above.

Eye beauty

Bags under the eyes

Alas, once that precious elasticity has been stretched out of the extra-delicate skin under the eyes so that it becomes loose and baggy, I'm afraid that it has gone for good and only the knife of a plastic surgeon can restore a certain smoothness—see **Plastic surgery** on page 63.

Eye creams

Unless you've found a product which doesn't affect you personally, (perhaps a natural rose geranium cream from a health store), never leave cream or oil round your eyes overnight or they'll be all puffed up by the morning.

Lashes

A smear of castor oil on lashes before applying mascara will encourage them to grow. But remember, don't leave any oil on overnight as your eyes are likely to puff up. If the mascara drifts with the oil underneath, a touch of powder over the oiled lashes before applying mascara should put this right—and thicken your lashes at the same time.

Make-up

Lots of hints about eye make-up in the *Make-up* section, pages 64—66.

Refreshers

Close your eyes whenever you can—apparently 80 per cent of our energy escapes through our eyes. But tired eyes also need exercising so when you're watching television or reading blink your eyes a number of times in succession as often as you think of it. Another excellent eye exercise is to keep your head still but roll your eyes round in a wide circle, first to the right, then to the left. Repeat a few times.

A cucumber slice laid over closed lids revives tired eyes.

To de-puff eyes after crying, peel and grate a medium-sized potato. Put the gratings on two bits of gauze and shape them into eyepatches. Lie down and place these on closed lids for ten minutes, or more if you want to. When you get up, sloosh lots of running water over your eyes to get rid of the starch. Pat dry, and put some moisturiser under your eyes.

Tea-bags, strained and left in the fridge, make cool, soothing eye refreshers.

Hand beauty

Our hands lead a very hard-working life, but there's no need for them to look rough and work-worn if you look after them regularly. Use a hand-lotion at night and after all wet jobs; make a point of keeping nails and cuticles in good trim.

Hand lotions

Here are a few you can make yourself:

1 Equal parts of glycerine and rosewater.

2 Two parts glycerine to one part fresh lemon juice.

3 Take equal parts of glycerine, methylated spirit and milk. Shake them up well and store in a glass container. This is a good softener for all rough skin areas—elbows, knees and so on, as well as hands—and will keep indefinitely despite the milk.

4 A really concentrated hand nourisher: the white of an egg, 1 teaspoonful glycerine, 1 ounce honey and enough ground barley to mix into a paste.

Manicure sets

Some manufacturers do put the right things into manicure sets, but most include metal files and prodders and no metal should be used on any but the strongest nails. A 'do it yourself' hands and feet kit should include:

orange sticks to clean nails
one orange stick with rubber 'hoof' to lift cuticles
emery boards
a buffer to make your nails shine and activate the circulation
cuticle clippers – but only if you're an expert

Nail care

Brittle, peeling and split nails are such a problem these days that it's well worth eating kelp and pollen capsules daily or just plain kelp tablets (all health stores stock these). And from America comes the gelatine cure which has helped many: dissolve three level teaspoonsful of gelatine either in cold fruit juice or a cup of hot soup and drink it down. I've known both remedies to be extremely successful over a month or so, but if you have a tendency to weak nails you'll have to keep it up.

Cuticles   Nails 'breathe' and 'eat' through the cuticles only, so keep them lifted and soft – massage any treatment cream well into the base of the nail. Some friends say that a half-and-half mixture of white iodine and almond oil well shaken and painted on nightly encourages nails to grow long and strong.

Instead of cutting cuticles, ask your chemist for a cuticle dissolving lotion. Roll a little cotton wool round the tip of an orange stick, dip it in the liquid and coax the cuticle off that way.

Filing   If your nails aren't too strong, always file them with the *fine* side of an emery board and don't draw any file backwards and forwards across the tips – file one way only.

Strengthening nails   A strengthener which stops my nails flaking and encourages them to grow: half a teaspoonful of castor oil well shaken up in an 8 ounce bottle of surgical spirit. I put a little of this mixture in two small screw-top jars, one in the kitchen and one in the bathroom, then dip my finger tips in it every time I've washed and dried my hands. A bit of a nuisance, but results usually make it worthwhile.

You can protect fragile nails, too, by using a pen or pencil to dial telephone numbers.

Varnish   A touch of white vinegar or lemon on nails before applying base coat and varnish will help your manicure last longer.

If you've run out of a quick-dry spray, nail varnish sets fast if you dip your fingertips into cold water for a few minutes.

Plastic surgery

Plastic surgery is a surgical speciality in its own right, which deals mainly with cancer, burns, congenital deformities and so on, and there is a plastic surgeon attached to most large hospitals to deal with the many accidents which need his immediate attention.

One branch of plastic surgery embraces the purely cosmetic plastic surgery, and these are some (superficial) facts about it.

To get in touch with a plastic surgeon, you must go through a general practitioner. This is an unwaivable rule of medical etiquette; the main object is to protect the patient from unqualified practitioners, and it also incidentally protects both the surgeon, who can then rely on the GP's summing up of the patient's general and mental health, and the GP, who has to recommend a fully trained surgeon, who in most cases is also a member of the British Association of Plastic Surgeons. A woman should have no problems discussing her wish to undergo plastic surgery with her GP. If, however, as often seems to be the case, she fears that he'll dismiss the idea as frivolous vanity, there's nothing to stop her taking her problems to another, more understanding GP.

Although plastic surgery is undertaken automatically to remedy the effects of an accident, it would be wise – if this applies to you – to look into your insurance policy. In the case of a car crash, for instance, you should be able to insist on the insurance company paying should any plastic surgery be needed.

Cosmetic plastic surgery can be performed under the National Health Service in certain individual cases, if the condition is proved to be harmful to the patient. For instance, eye surgery will be accepted by the NHS if a person's vision is obstructed. Generally, however, you will have to have cosmetic surgery done privately, and pay accordingly. The fees vary so much that I won't even quote approximate figures.

We all age at a different rate, so that every case must be judged on its own merits, but for the most effective and lasting results it is generally accepted that one shouldn't undergo plastic surgery at the first sign of a sagging jawline. If in doubt, ask your GP to arrange an appointment with a plastic surgeon so that you can ask his advice, without any commitment to undergo surgery at that stage.

Before operating, a plastic surgeon will want to explain to you what the operation will involve. He will also want to know of your experiences with cuts and bruises, and inspect scars from any previous operations or accidents you may have had. This is because people vary tremendously in how they heal, and a plastic surgeon may even refuse to operate if he thinks a kiloid (raised, uneven scar tissue) may form and destroy the whole point of a particular operation. During this session don't be shy about discussing fees and asking any and every question that worries you.

The more usual types of plastic surgery and what they involve

Breast surgery   Breasts can be increased as well as reduced in size. Opinions are still divided as to whether or not they should be enlarged, on account of possible side effects, but the surgeons who agree to do this operation insert silicone or saline-filled sacks through an incision in the natural fold under the breasts. To make a bust smaller, excess fat is shredded through various incisions underneath the breasts, and in some cases the nipples have to be placed in a different position. This operation does leave scars, so only women with uncomfortably outsize breasts should contemplate it.

Chin re-shaping   This is usually done to remedy a receding chin, which is built up with silastic, a synthetic, slightly spongey material. The stitching is done inside the mouth, mostly with soluble gut, so there are no or very few stitches to take out and there is little visible bruising and swelling. The patient is out of action for about a week.

Complete face lift   This operation lifts slack skin, smooths the jawline and cheeks, takes away the mouth-to-nose lines and improves the neck, all at the same time. As you can imagine, it's a big job. The incisions are made in front and behind the ears as well as on the scalp. There's no need to be shorn of hair, in fact it's better to wear a longish style so as to hide the incisions near the ears while they are healing. Stitches come out after eight to ten days, but you'll want to stay out of sight for about a fortnight. This operation can be done more than once, but when to have the first one depends on the individual and varies tremendously. Certainly not at the first blurring of the jawline.

Eyes   The most usual operation is to remove bags and lift droopy lids. In Britain a general anaesthetic is nearly always used so that the patient is completely relaxed and the surgeon can take his time. Bandages in the shape of a blindfold are left on overnight, because if the tissue is kept really still at the start there'll be less bruising and the scars will heal quicker. The patient spends three to five days in hospital, and the stitches come out after approximately five to seven days. Bruises last for about ten days, but after about nine days make-up can be worn, which, together with dark glasses, will camouflage any leftover yellowish tinges and disguise a faint redness over the eyes which may last for three weeks after that.

Nose shaping   This is still the most frequently sought-after cosmetic operation. The surgeon likes first to study pictures of the sort of nose you'd like to have, considering it and adapting it in relation to the shape and size of your face and other features. The operation is performed from inside the nose and a plaster cast holds the new outline in place for a week to ten days. By this time most of the bruising will have gone. Usually four to five nights will have to be spent in hospital.

Other parts of the body General tuck-ins can be performed on inner thighs, bottoms, flabby under-arms and tummies. As plastic surgery scars should ideally be hidden in a natural body 'pleat', such operations are most successful where these 'pleats' are most obvious. Surgeons insist on their patients losing as much weight as possible before operating so that there's more skin than fat to take away. 'Kimono' or 'bat-wing' arms will show a fine scar on the inner arm. Baggy skin on the tummy due to pregnancies or considerable weight fluctuations can be tidied up but there will be a scar left. There are no general rules as to how long a patient has to stay in hospital: this depends on the surgeon, the work needed, and the individual's reactions.

Please don't write to me for the name of a plastic surgeon. Much as I would like to help you, I repeat, you have got to be introduced through a GP.

Make-up

A fresh look at your make-up can give a fresh look to your face. I've lots of ideas here on eyebrows, eyes, foundation and power, lipstick — and your make-up tools, very important!

Points to remember when you're making up: never drag the skin when applying or removing make-up and creams — remember that the skin's elasticity is irreplaceable, once gone it is gone forever. Always make-up if possible in the harshest of natural daylight. Don't stop make-up sharply along the jaw, take it down into the neck. And I can't stress strongly enough the importance of blending all shades and colours with subtlety — without this the effect can be distinctly clownlike.

Eyebrows

Plucking A face will look younger and more alive if the outer edges of the brows tend to go upwards. Unless you want to look hard and older, don't accentuate any natural downward curve — if your brows are that way inclined, just pluck them slightly at the ends and feather them outwards towards the hair-line.

Get a firm grip on the tweezers and tweak in the direction the hair grows in, not against it, or the hair will probably snap without the roots coming out. A touch of surgical spirit on the skin before you start plucking both soothes and disinfects. If you can't do it facing the harsh white daylight, then face the mirror with a strong lamp bulb under your chin — gruesomely revealing, but that's what you need.

The best shape of eyebrow plucker is the one you prefer. After much trial and error I find I like the very flat ones with rounded ends.

Using eyebrow pencils Always 'feather' in eyebrows with short, fly-away strokes which you can continue if you want to extend the brows where the hair is extra sparse. A blunt pencil is more practical for this than a sharply-pointed one, but always choose a soft-leaded one. Now brush over what you have feathered with a hard mascara brush, and the effect will be surprisingly natural.

By the way, soft eyebrow pencils will sharpen easily if first left to harden in the freezer or ice compartment of the fridge.

Eyes

To camouflage dark shadows under the eyes, apply lightly with your fingertip a very pale cover cream and blend in edges with your other foundation. Let this settle in before dusting sparingly with a translucent powder. If your cover cream doesn't flow on effortlessly, a touch of moisture cream on your finger before you put on the camouflaging one — this will make it easier to smooth on.

Eye liner To make your lashes look even thicker, frame your eyes by drawing a narrow line as near the roots of the lashes as possible with a soft black pencil. Then, using a small but firm-tipped brush, smudge the edges of this line with powdered eyeshadow (blue, green or whatever you fancy) and blend in with your eye make-up of the moment.

Eye pencils If you like to use make-up pencils on your lids, make sure they're super soft and not too sharp. If you drag anything across the skin you'll use up that precious elasticity.

Mascara will look thicker if you fluff a touch of powder with a thick brush over the first coating before it's quite dry, and mascara again at once. If you want a very thick fringe of lashes, keep re-applying the mascara just before the previous layer has dried. If you wait for it to dry before adding the next coating, the effect will be spiky.

Never go to bed without taking off your mascara — if you do, the lashes will become brittle and snap. Taking off mascara leaves most eyes red for a few minutes, but they should then settle down with no discomfort. I have extremely delicate eyes, but I use both liquid eye make-up remover and eye make-up removing pads with equal success.

With the liquid remover or removing pads, soak a small pad of cotton wool and stroke it downwards over closed lids and lashes a number of times, then open your eyes and stroke, even more gently so as not to stretch that delicate skin area, underneath the lashes, from the corners inwards. Now bend over the hand basin and with a clean pad of cotton wool sloosh lots of tepid running water over the eyes to remove the final traces of mascara. If your eyes feel gritty, wash them out in eye lotion in an eye-bath and rest a cold tea bag on each lid before going to sleep.

Short-sighted? You can still use eye make-up, even if you can't see properly without glasses — that is, if you've kept a couple of pairs of old spectacles. Carefully cut the frame of one pair in half, leaving the nose piece on the right-hand side, then cut the other pair leaving the left-hand piece on it. Now you've got a sort of monocle for each eye, and you can make up the left eye whilst wearing the right-hand monocle and vice versa.

What shape are your eyes? How you make up your eyes must depend on their shape. Fashions in eye make-up change quicker than it takes to blink, but here are some general guidelines which should always be useful.

 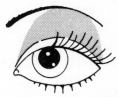

Deep-set eyes need a very pale coloured shading on the actual lid to make them more noticeable, and a soft but dark colour from socket to eyebrow will increase the illusion.

 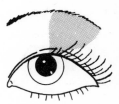

Droopy-ended eyes can be lifted by not putting any shading on the outer edges of the eyes. Concentrate instead on applying colour from the centre lid upwards to the brow and then outwards only *on* the actual brow bone. Lift the eyebrows, too, by plucking away any downward stragglers and feathering in an outward direction towards the hairline.

Pop-eyes can look deeper set with a soft, dark shading all over the actual lid and a really pale colour applied from the socket up to the eyebrow will accentuate the effect further.

Too close together eyes will appear further apart by blending a touch of pale or white shadow into the inner corners of the eye, and even up the sides of the nose – any colour should be put on the outer edges of the eye and brow. You can also pluck a few hairs between the brows so as to widen the space above the bridge of the nose.

Too narrow eyes need rounding and 'opening', so use lots of mascara on both top and bottom lashes and smudge in a little eyeshadow under the bottom lashes, as well as on the lids. Shape the brows with a 'lifted' curve.

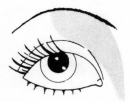 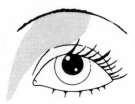  

Too far apart eyes (don't worry, it shows you've got a generous nature) can be brought closer together by shading right into the corners of the eyes, and even in extreme cases down each side of the bridge of the nose. You can also bring the eyebrows closer in by feathering a few extra hairs where they start above the nose.

Too round eyes need to be given an almond shape, so start with eye liner and blend the shading from the centre of the lid outwards, deepening the colour at the outer edge of the eye and upwards towards the brow. Pluck the eyebrows into a sharper arch, but be careful not to give yourself a permanently surprised expression!

Foundation and powder

Foundation   Tinted foundations were invented because the majority of us look pretty colourless without a little help—choose a base which is slightly stronger than your natural skin tone but which blends in with it best. The back of your hand is not the best area for trying out make-up, as it can be windswept and work-worn, but as skin textures and areas vary tremendously from one individual to the next, put the palm of your hand up to your face, and pick the skin shade which most resembles your complexion, but you may find the jawline and neck are better testing grounds.

If you've bought a liquid foundation which turns out to be too pale, stir in some creamy liquid rouge to give it more warmth. Again blend the foundation down over your jawline and onto your neck.

Powder   Neutral translucent powder won't give an over-matt look or clog the skin, but will 'set' a base and prolong any effect you aim for. Always fluff it on downwards, because that's the direction in which natural facial 'down' grows.

Old-fashioned swansdown puffs are worth hunting for because they fluff on less powder than anything else—but thick, chunky, soft-tufted brushes are the best alternative. If you use cotton wool, press with a sort of rocking movement on the shiny areas.

For that extra natural look, after you've powdered press a tissue dampened and wrung out in cool water gently over your finished make-up.

Shading   Shade the parts of your face you want 'overlooked', lighten and brighten the ones you want to accentuate. So cheekbones will look higher with a touch of colour—just under the outer corners of the eyes, blended out towards the hairline. The fattest cheeks can be slimmed by a curve of shading just where they should sink in. Suck in your cheeks—that'll give you the right line. A touch of shading at the tip of the nose will shorten it; a stripe of blusher down each side will make it look slimmer. And you can give yourself a smoother jawline by drawing a straight line along the bone with a brownish blusher—but take care to blend it in with your make-up and below the jaw so as to avoid that demarcation give-away.

Lipsticks

Make your own lipstick   If, like lots of people I know, you have a collection of nearly finished lipsticks, scoop them out and put them into a small screw-top glass jar. You'll have great fun and save money mixing and matching them with your lip-brush.

Smudging   Different lipsticks will sometimes drift on different people—but this method of applying the colour nearly always stops this: dab a little foundation over your lip line, blot with a tissue, then use a lip *pencil*—not a brush—to give a slight outline to the top lip before filling in with the lipstick itself.
Lipgloss often encourages lipstick to drift over the lip edges, so make sure to keep the gloss away from the lip outline.

Make-up 'tools'

Cleanliness   Do keep all make-up 'tools' scrupulously clean—wash brushes often—particularly important this; if a person is prone to getting spots, it'll avoid spreading infection.

Cotton wool   A large roll of 'surgery' cotton wool costs less than half what 'best' cotton wool does, and works just as well at the dressing table.

If you unwind a roll of cotton wool and hang it over a warm radiator for an hour or so, it will expand; then you can separate it into layers and it'll go twice as far.

Cotton wool buds are useful make-up repairers, especially when mascara drifts.

Containers   Most tubes as well as bottles of creams and make-up balance quite steadily on their screw tops, so just stand them upside down and you'll be able to use them down to the last drop.

Plastic food containers on planes usually get chucked out with the rubbish after a flight anyway, so rescue them—the more solid ones—they make excellent make-up containers for dressing table drawers.

Tissues   One tissue usually separates into two layers, so a box will last twice as long if you do this — and if you can get over any mental block, soft loo paper works just as well as tissues and is cheaper.

Nail varnish   When you've used your nail varnish, wipe the bottle top and screw-liner very thoroughly with a tissue soaked in remover (not cotton wool, which will leave 'bits'), then you'll have no trouble unscrewing it next time.

Just for fun
Bits and pieces

Here are some bits and pieces of information . . . just for fun.

How to address a married woman?   Women's Libbers may not agree, but lots of others may still like to know that on an envelope a married woman should always be addressed as 'Mrs' followed by her husband's name or initial, and then his surname. If she is widowed, she is still entitled to this style of address. When 'Mrs' is followed by the lady's own Christian name or initial, it means she's divorced.

How to make a pot pourri?   Literally, *pot pourri* is French for a pot of things which have gone bad, and it's a collection of dried flowers, petals, leaves and herbs blended with special oils. A prowl round your local library should unearth books with old recipes, but there are endless permutations you can concoct from already packaged basic ingredients to be bought at most health food shops or department stores complete with suggested recipes. To prepare your own petals and herbs, make sure they're picked in healthy bloom and dry them — away from the light, or they'll lose their colour — between sheets of newspapers laid on a tray in a not-too-warm airing cupboard. A sprinkling of salt, borax or silversand will help to dehydrate them.

How to stop hiccups?   The most reliable way needs the help of a friend. Put your fingers in your ears so that you really can't hear a thing, and get your friend to hold your nose while giving you a glass of water to sip. When you feel you'll burst, give your friend the wink and get unplugged! I guarantee no more hiccups — but even if there was one left, you'd have had a giggle.

Other hiccuping remedies I've seen work are sipping a teaspoonful of neat vinegar, sipping a glass of water from the wrong side — or rolling up the shirt-sleeves of the hiccupper, very slowly from wrist to shoulder. No kidding. Try it and see.

How to work out time differences throughout the world? One revolution of the earth (that is, one day) takes twenty-four hours, so the earth turns 360 degrees in that time, which is 15 degrees every hour. Thus a place 15 degrees east of Greenwich will be one hour ahead of GMT and a place 30 degrees east will be two hours ahead. A place 30 degrees west will be two hours behind, and so on. Now go to your atlas, check your longitudes and take it from there.

The Queen's telegram can be solicited only for hundredth birthdays, diamond weddings or multiple births from triplets upwards. Relatives should apply to the Secretary, Buckingham Palace, London SW1.

Why do people across the channel cross their sevens? This custom stems from the original Arabic numbering system, where the mathematical Arabic race invented figures with as many angles as the number itself. The figures were as follows (the angles shown by the dots):

In usage, the symbols became rounded off into curves and the seven lost its cross in some countries as the Arabic origins were gradually forgotten. The Continentals kept the cross so it didn't get muddled with the 'ones'.

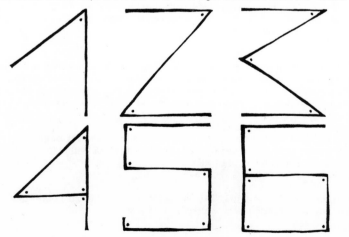

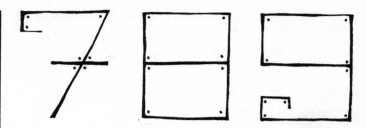

Why we must dial 999 in an emergency instead of the obviously quicker 111? According to the Post Office, when the Emergency Service was introduced in 1937, the only codes feasible were those containing 9 and 0. The code 111 was considered, but rejected because outside wires tapping together or a customer accidentally knocking his telephone could cause a false alarm. With modern call-boxes and greater use of underground cabling, some of the original reasons for choosing 999 no longer apply, but the Post Office argue that as the public is so used to it any change would only cause confusion. What's more, it in fact only takes three seconds longer to dial 999 than 111, so little time is lost—and it's just as easy to dial in the dark.

The Willow Pattern story Many homes have Willow Pattern china. This is the fable surrounding it.

A rich Mandarin lives in a tall house with a beautiful garden, and employs a young scribe called Chang, who falls in love with the Mandarin's daughter, Koong-see. But the father disapproves; he sacks Chang and bethrothes Koong-see to a rich old duke, Ta-jen, and keeps her confined in the house and garden. One day, Koong-see notices a half coconut shell floating in the stream: inside is a message from Chang, saying he will come back to fetch her. Soon after this, Ta-jen visits the Mandarin with jewels for his future bride, and while the two old men are celebrating over wine, Chang slips into the house unnoticed. Chang and Koong-see escape across the little bridge over the stream with her father in hot pursuit. The couple hide and live happily for a while, until Ta-jen finds them. He hires soldiers who mortally wound Chang. Koong-see flees to their home, sets it on fire and dies in the flames. In revenge, the gods curse the wicked Ta-jen with a fatal disease, and transform the two lovers into immortal doves.

The first Willow Pattern china was produced in England in 1780 by Minton, but lots of china manufacturers have made it since and the pattern varies slightly between them. Most of the designs, though, show the tall house, the garden, the bridge with three figures on it and the two doves fluttering away.

Origins of words, sayings and superstitions

Abracadabra   The magician's exclamation was originally a word charm made up of the Hebrew words Ab (Father), Ben (Son), and Ruach Acadsch (Holy Spirit), and used against sickness and pain. It was written on a triangle of parchment and hung round the neck on a linen thread.

```
ABRACADABRA
ABRACADABR
ABRACADAB
ABRACADA
ABRACAD
ABRACA
ABRAC
ABRA
ABR
AB
A
```

Adam's apple   The bump in a man's throat is so called because a lump of the forbidden apple is supposed to have stuck there on the way down. He probably had a guilty conscience. We women have smooth throats — no comment!

An axe to grind   A man wanted to grind an axe but couldn't be bothered to turn the grindstone. He saw young Benjamin Franklin in a yard and asked the boy to show him how the machine worked. As the boy sharpened the man's axe, the man praised his skill, but when it was finished he laughed at young Franklin for taking all that trouble. The expression still stands for someone who has an ulterior, selfish motive.

Barking up the wrong tree   Racoon hunting always took place at night and dogs barked under the trees where the racoons were hiding. But sometimes they got the wrong trees in the dark — therefore wasting energy after the wrong scent.

A blue stocking is a synonym for brains usually accompanied by drabness of dress. In Venice in 1400 learned men and women who cared little for the fripperies of fashion formed a society and were distinguished by the dull blue stockings they wore. The Society in fact was called 'della Calza' ('of the stocking'). A similar society was the rage amongst intellectual females in Paris in 1590. A Mrs Montagu founded another, based on that one, in Britain in 1750, and a prominent member, Mr Benjamin Stillingfleet, always wore blue stockings. The last prominent member was a Miss Monckton, later Countess of Cork, who died in 1840.

Breaking a mirror   The superstition that this is unlucky stems from the days when magicians used mirrors as a predecessor to the crystal ball to give answers when telling fortunes. If one got broken the enquirer's questions had to stay unanswered.

A dying duck in a thunderstorm describes someone who is woebegone, because young ducks catch cold and die very easily if caught outside in a sudden downpour.

Eating humble pie   Humble is a play of words on 'umbles', which are the heart, liver and entrails of the deer. After the hunt when the lord of the manor and his friends used to dine off the venison on a dais, the huntsmen sat on a lower level and ate pie made of the umbles.

A feather in your cap, meaning a personal achievement, originated with the custom American Indians had of adding an extra feather to their headgear for every enemy they killed.

A hair of the dog that bit you goes back to the old notion that the burnt hair of a dog is an antidote to its bite.

In the bag   Anyone wanting to present a petition to Parliament has to have it put in the big canvas bag which hangs behind the Speaker's chair in the House of Commons. So the expression implies optimistically that something is as good as done.

In the doghouse   It was Mr Darling who lived in the dog kennel as a penance until his children came back, for his treatment of the family dog, Nana, who tried to warn him about Peter, in J. M. Barrie's *Peter Pan*.

Keeping one's fingers crossed   The sign of the cross protects us, so by crossing our fingers we hopefully ensure against disaster.

Kiss the place and make it better   A leftover from the custom of sucking poison out of wounds. And also in memory of St Martin of Tours, who went over to a leper and kissed his sores, whereupon the leper immediately became whole again.

Lemon sole has nothing to do with a lemon, but comes from the French limande, meaning a flat board, or maybe even the Latin, *limus*, meaning mud, because the sole is a bottom-of-the-sea fish.

The leopard can't change his spots   This comes from Shakespeare's Richard II (II.1.i):

King Richard: Lions make leopards tame.
Duke of Norfolk: Yea, but not change his spots.

That is, what's bred in the bone is there for keeps.

Little pitchers have big ears refers to children listening to adult conversations, and comes from the fact that small mugs and beakers often used to have handles made in the shape of a large ear.

Lost in the wash   This expression alludes to the loss of King John's luggage and treasure in 1216, when his convoy was caught and swallowed up by the tide on the sands of the Wash.

Love is blind because Cupid, the Roman god of love (Eros is the Greek) is always represented as a beautiful winged boy, with a bow and arrows, but blindfolded.

A nine day's wonder comes from the old proverb: 'A wonder lasts nine days, and then the puppy's eyes are open.' In other words, the public's eyes are blinded by astonishment for nine days, but then, with open eyes, they see too much to wonder any longer.

A nip...of whisky, gin, etc is an abbreviation of nipperkin, which is a small wine and beer measure of about half a pint or a little less.

Not dry behind the ears means as innocent as a new-born babe, because the last place to dry off on a newly born animal is a little indentation behind the ears.

Not fit to hold a candle to him This dates back to the young boys who held candles in theatres and other places of night entertainment long before the days of electricity.

Not for donkey's years means not for ages, because of the old tradition that one never sees a dead donkey.

The pawnbroker's sign of three golden balls was taken from the arms of the Duke of Medici and introduced to London by moneylenders and bankers from Lombardy in Italy. The balls in that position are supposed to mean that there are two chances to one that what is given to the pawnbroker won't be redeemed. The three golden balls are also the emblem of Saint Nicholas of Bari, Italy, who is supposed to have given three purses of gold to three virgin sisters so that they could get married.

To pay with the roll of the drum means not to pay at all, because no soldier can be arrested for debt when he's on the march.

Pin money This now means a woman's small allowance, or pocket money, but the expression dates back to the fourteenth and fifteenth centuries when pins were extremely expensive and special bequests in wills were worded 'for the express purpose of the beneficiary to buy pins'. Pins became cheaper, but the expression lingered on, so that pin money now means a pittance.

Plain sailing should be spelt *plane*, because it comes from planning a ship's course in the days when it was thought the earth was flat, and the computing of distances was quite straightforward – plane sailing.

Poor as a church mouse There's no pantry in a church, so the mice there have a lean time.

A quack doctor In the middle ages, pedlars of potions at fairs 'quacked' long and loud about their healing powers to hoodwink the public into buying them.

Raining cats and dogs This comes from northern mythology. The cat is greatly influenced by the weather, and when she was unusually frisky seafarers used to say 'She has a gale in her tail'; added to this, witches who rode the storm were supposed to take the form of a cat. The dog and the wolf were symbols of wind and attendants on Odin, the storm-god. So the cat represents down-pouring rain and the dog the gusts of wind that went with it.

Reading between the lines A method of coding is to send a message which only makes sense when alternate lines are read.

Ring a ring of roses This old nursery rhyme has gruesome roots. Way back at the time of the Plague of London, the skin of plague victims erupted in small red circles which looked like a 'ring of roses'. 'A pocketful of posies' was carried to counteract the unpleasant smell the plague brought with it, and the day before the victim died, bad bouts of sneezing warned him of his imminent fate.

See Naples and die   Naples was once the centre of typhoid and cholera, incurable diseases at the time, so if you went there you were likely to catch either or both and die. Fact tends to be less romantic than fiction!

Setting her cap at him   In the days when hats were the rage a lady would naturally put on her very prettiest to attract the attention of the man she wanted.

The skeleton at the feast   Plutarch tells that the Egyptians had a skeleton sitting at all their banquets to remind them that there are inevitably troubles as well as pleasure in life.

The skeleton in the cupboard   There was a story that in days gone by, someone had to be found with no troubles or cares in the world. At last a woman appeared who seemed to be the perfect candidate — until she went upstairs, opened a cupboard and revealed a skeleton which her husband insisted that she should kiss each night. He was once her husband's rival and was shot in a duel. Which proves that *everyone* has their troubles, hidden or otherwise.

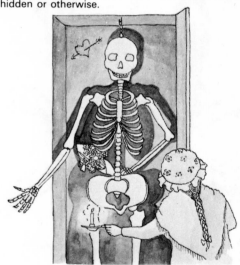

Skull and crossbones   These were shown on the priates' flag as a symbol of mortality. The crossed bones are two thigh bones laid one across the other.

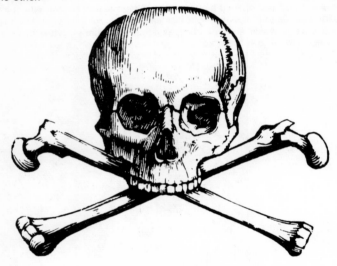

Soldiers of fortune were those in medieval times who hired themselves out to any army.

To turn over a new leaf   Before the invention of paper, the leaves of certain plants were used for writing on, and the derivation of the word 'paper' itself comes from papyrus, the giant water reed which the Egyptians made into a writing material. The double page of a ledger is still called a folio – Latin for 'leaf'.

Useful addresses

Where to go for help

ANZEFA
Ludgate House
107 Fleet Street
London EC4
Tel: 01-353 5786

The Australian and New Zealand immigrant Families Association.

The Association of British Adoption Agencies
4 Southampton Row
London WC1B 4AA
Tel: 01-242 8951

This Association co-ordinates all adoption societies around Britain.

Agoraphobia – The Open Door
Mrs Neville
4 Manorbrook
Blackheath
London SE3

This organisation helps the many people who are made prisoners in their own home, by their obsessive fear of going into open places.

Alcoholics Anonymous
11 Redcliffe Gardens
London SW10
Tel: 01-352 9669

They'll help to restrain the obsessive love of the bottle.

Al-Anon Family Groups
c/o St Giles Centre
Camberwell Church Street
London SE5 8R8
Tel: 01-703 0397

These groups consist of relatives and friends of alcoholics who, by banding together, can better solve the problems they share. For their leaflets write to them direct.

Citizens Advice Bureau
There are over 600 of these all over the country. Just look up your nearest branch in the telephone directory. Their staff, 90 per cent volunteers, 10 per cent salaried, go through a training course, followed up by refresher courses from time to time. So if you're in doubt about *anything*, whether it be how to get legal aid, make a will, muddle out your income tax, hire purchases, fill in a form, write a complicated official letter, fight with your neighbour, etc etc, ask them. If they don't know the answer themselves, they'll direct you to someone who does.

National Council for the Divorced and Separated
Grove House
Steeple Bumpstead
Suffolk

The Council's aims are to help people whose marriages have ended in divorce or separation, and provide information and opinions on matters of concern to those people. The Association brings out frequent news bulletins and has had its first welfare conference. It's worth getting in touch with them for all information and for the address of your nearest club. But *please* don't forget to include a SAE! There are Clubs affiliated with NCDs all over Britain.

The National Marriage Guidance Council
Head Office
Little Church Street
Rugby, Warwickshire
Rugby 73241

They have 400 branches in Britain, and you'll find your nearest in the telephone book, or at the library. All marriages go through bad patches. Instead of going to the divorce court, get in with a marriage counsellor; they are not only trained but sympathetic and keep all secrets.

National Council for One-Parent Families
(*formerly National Council for the Unmarried Mother and her Child*)
255 Kentish Town Road
London NW5 2LX
Tel: 01-267 1361

Their aim is to help lone parents solve problems in all fields – legal, schooling, housing, financial etc – and inform them of the legal rights and social facilities that exist for them.

Gingerbread
An Association for One-Parent Families
9 Poland Street
London W1V 3DG
Tel: 01-734 9014

With branches sprouting up all over Britain — very friendly and welcoming.

The National Council for the Single Woman and Her Dependents
166 Victoria Street
London SW1E 5BR
Tel: 01-828 5511

40 branches throughout Britain, again help solve problems in all fields — legal, schooling, housing, financial, etc — whether the parent be divorced, separated, widowed, single or a 'prison or hospital widow or widower'. Write to London H.Q. for the address of your nearest branch.

Cruse
(National Organisation for Widows and their Children)
Cruse House
126 Sheen Road
Richmond
Surrey
Tel: 01-940 4818

The functions of this club are many and varied but all are directed towards giving support to the widowed family, especially the widowed mother. The director sends out a very useful monthly newsletter as well as interesting leaflets full of advice for the widowed mother. Write to them for full details.

Salvation Army Missing Persons Bureau
110 Middlesex Street
London E1 7HX
Tel: 01-247 6831

They'll try to trace lost relatives and friends, asking small donation towards costs. Private detective agencies do this job too ... at a price.

Samaritans
When personal problems seem to be too hard to bear, ring them. They have branches all over the country. You can find them in your phone book.

Medic Alert
9 Hanover Street
London W1R 9HF
Tel: 01-499 2261

They supply discs to identify sufferers for particular illnesses which need special attention in case of accident.

National Association for Gifted Children
27 John Adam Street
London WC2
Tel: 01-930 7731

Even parents of brilliantly clever children have their problems and this Association will help to solve them.

National Association for the Care and Resettlement of Offenders
125 Kennington Park Road
London SE7

When someone has had a spell 'inside', they need all the sympathetic help they can be given.

Pregnancy and contraception

The Family Planning Association
If you feel you cannot first approach your family doctor, the Association, which has 30 branches and over 900 clinics throughout Britain, will give advice to single as well as married women. Their specialist staff will advise on all methods of birth control and are never too busy to discuss any problem.

The Pregnancy Advisory Service
40 Margaret Street
London W1N 7SB
Tel: 01-629 9575

The Midland Pregnancy Advisory Service
109 Gough Road
Edgbaston
Birmingham 15
Tel: 021-440 2570

Pregnancy Information Centre
Suite B., Dept. N
Chicago Buildings
Whitechapel
Liverpool 1
Tel: 051-236 8668

If you are pregnant, or are worried about becoming so, these three addresses will treat your worry sympathetically.

Brook Advisory Centre
233 Tottenham Court Road
London W1P 9NE
Tel: 01-323 1522
    01-580 2991

Brook have 19 centres throughout the UK and give advice and practical help on birth control, as well as help on emotional or sexual problems. Write off for their explanatory leaflet which also gives details of your nearest clinic. Brook is a registered charity and advice is free.

Retirement and old age

Age Concern
Bernard Sunley House
60 Pitcairn Road
Mitcham
Surrey CR4 3LL
Tel: 01-947 3671

Full of practical ideas and advice for the senior citizen.

Old People's Welfare Department of your local authority
OAPs should keep in touch with this Welfare Department because they can organise special facilities such as:

Home helps, loan of home nursing equipment, chiropody, special laundry services, rent-free telephones (in certain cases), extra heating allowances, aids for the partially-sighted or deaf, concessionary travel passes, cheap holidays, luncheon clubs, 'cookery in retirement' courses, part-time employment, WRVS Darby-and-Joan Clubs and meals-on-wheels, sheltered housing, residential homes, advice on claiming supplementary benefits, rent or rates rebates, tax concessions, cheaper shopping, ancient local charities for elderly people, etc etc.

The Old People's Information Service
10 Fleet Street
London EC4
Tel: 01-353 1892

For a list of useful books on the subject of retirement and how to spend it happily, write off to this Service.

SAGA
Senior Citizens Holidays
119 Sandgate Road
Folkestone, Kent
Tel: 0303 57300

SAGA specialise in UK and continental tours. Their 'holidays for only ones' organise social events in order for the holidaymakers to get to know each other. *Saga News* is published quarterly with new holidays advertised.

The Sundial Society
3 Perrycroft
Windsor
Berks
Tel: Windsor 67854

This association is for senior citizens who wish to extend their circle of friends and to develop new ideas. There are small groups within the Society who share the same interests such as reading, writing, gardening, painting, discussion etc.

Cape Grapes for Centenarians
7 Staple Inn
Holborn
London WC1V 7QH

Sent free as a 100th birthday present.

Helping youth

The Sports Council
70 Brompton Road
London SW3 1EX
Tel: 01-589 3411

For information on all sports either as a watcher or a doer.

National Federation of Eighteen-Plus Groups
16/18 High Street
Dartford
Kent
Tel: Dartford 23591

The Club's aims are to cater for the members' individual interests. Have 200 groups throughout England with plans in hand for Scotland and South Wales.

The Young People's Advisory Service
34 Stanley Street
Liverpool 1
Tel: 051 236 6774

If not quite sure which career would suit you these knowledgeable people will come up with some carefully thought up suggestions according to your talents. They'll also guide you along the route by putting you in touch with the experts.

Grapevine
296 Holloway Road
London N7
Tel: 01-607 0949

This is a young people's information and advice service dealing primarily with relationships and (sexual) problems of the under-30s. Those who run Grapevine are young themselves so speak the same language as those they are there to help.

National Council for the Diploma in Art and Design
16 Park Crescent
London NW1
Tel: 01-580 1529

If you have ambitions to become a dress, costume or stage designer write for a list of art schools that teach these subjects.

Gabbitas-Thring Educational Trust
Broughton House
6–8 Sackville Street
Piccadilly, London W1X 2BR
Tel: 01-734 0161

A free advisory service on independent education. They come up with the answers on boarding schools in England and Europe – finishing schools and families, coaching establishments, secretarial colleges, domestic science colleges, correspondence courses, and courses on sailing, beauty culture, riding and many others. They solve many a problem for the school leaver and younger.

For the handicapped

The Social Services Department of the local council will always give help and information on everyday facilities provided for handicapped children, but you may also find the following names and addresses useful.

The local welfare officer in all areas deals with such things as adapting the lavatory (or loo) and bath so that a disabled person can use them without any help. One-handed table cutlery. Gadgets for putting on stockings and doing up zips, and for picking things up from the floor if you cannot bend. Visits from a district nurse, home help and the WRVS. Meals-on-wheels service can also often be arranged.

National Insurance Office
If a handicapped person needs constant care far above the normal, an attendance allowance should be applied for on Form DS 2C, obtainable from the local NIO. Part of it has to be filled in by a doctor, then the Attendance Allowance Board will decide whether or not the allowance can be granted.

The National Society for Mentally Handicapped Children
Pembridge Hall
17 Pembridge Square
London W2
Tel: 01-229 8941

and

5 Coventry Street (Metropolitan HQ)
London W1
Tel: 01-437 4538

Teaching, occupational and holiday establishments are built and staff trained to run them by this society. Write for details. Remember that SAE.

Royal National Institute for the Blind
224 Great Portland Street
London W1
Tel: 01-387 5571

The Royal National Institute for the Deaf
105 Gower Street
London W1
Tel: 01-387 8033

The National Listening Library
49 Great Cumberland Place
London W1M 7LM
Tel: 01-723 5008

Exists to supply 'talking books' (i.e. tape recording of books read aloud) for the handicapped.

General Welfare of the Blind
8/22 Curtain Road,
London EC2A 3NQ

The Disabled Living Foundation
346 Kensington High Street
London W14
Tel: 01-602 2491

and

18/19 Claremont Crescent
Edinburgh
Tel: 031-556 3882

This has local associations all over the country. It runs research projects on physical recreation, holidays and leisure activities, as well as on mechanical aids which help the disabled to do things for themselves.

The Central Council for the Disabled
34 Eccleston Square
London SW1
Tel: 01-834 0747

Among other things, they publish the Access guides which tell how the disabled can make use of public transport, cinemas, theatres, etc. Access can be ordered from the Central Council if you can't get it from your local book shop. Also published by them is *London for the Disabled* by Freda Bruce Lockhart.

Kermessee
Camden Lock
Chalk Farm Road
London NW1

Kermessee specialise in making toys and furniture for the individual needs of the handicapped.

The Joseph Rowntree Memorial Trust
Beverley House
Shipton Road
York YO3 6RB

This trust exists to help families who have a severely congenitally
handicapped child. The Fund is always anxious to consider new and
unusual ways of helping. If you would like further details, drop a note
to The Secretary for a copy of their leaflet *The Family Fund*.

Possum Users Association
Originally formed from the initials *POSM=Patient Operated Selector
Mechanism*. These are electronic aids which enable a severely disabled
person to operate by remote control a bell, buzzer alarm, light, heat,
radio, television (with channel change), intercom to front door, electric
door lock. Also a specially adapted loudspeaking telephone with
self-dialling system.

It can be adapted to electric typewriters and other equipment too so as
to help give a handicapped person as much independence as possible.
They have a magazine called *Possability* circulated to all members for
the exchange of information, advice, ideas etc. For details contact:

The Hon. Editor R. A. Bowell
Copper Beach
Parry's Close
Stoke Bishop
Bristol BS9 1AW

The Brittle Bone Club (Great Britain)
63 Byron Crescent
Dundee, Scotland DD3 6SS

The main purpose of the club is to put parents of children with this
handicap in touch with each other to exchange experience and advice.
But it also keeps in touch with the Institute of Orthopaedics in London
so that doctors can know of as many cases as possible and continue
their study of the cause of this disability.

British Dyslexia Association
18 The Circus
Bath BA1 2ET
Tel: Bath 20554

and

North London Dyslexia Association
78 Whitehall Park
London N19 3TN
Tel: 01-272 1331

Commonly known as 'word blindness' dyslexia is a severe difficulty in
learning to read and spell. The cause, which is not lack of intelligence,
has not been clearly established, but great progress has been made in
methods of teaching the dyslexic to overcome his disability.

If you are interested in social work

The Social Work Advisory Service
26 Bloomsbury Way
London WC1A 2SR
Tel: 01-242 5654

A *paid job* in Social Service does entail a training period. The Advisory
Service will send you all the details.

The National Council of Social Services
26 Bedford Square
London WC1
Tel: 01-636 4066

For voluntary or part-time social service it's best to go to your local
Citizens Advice Bureau for details of local projects or write to the
National Council.

For pet owners

Rules about the importing of animals and a list of quarantine kennels
and catteries are available from:
The Ministry of Agriculture, Fisheries and Food
Government Buildings
Hook Rise South
Tolworth, Surbiton, Surrey
Tel: 01-337 6611

To find out where you can get a specific breed of dog, write for the addresses of breeders to:

The Kennel Club
1 Clarges Street
London W1

Breeders' addresses can also be found in publications such as *Our Dogs*, *Dog News*, etc, available from most bookstalls.

The National Dog Owners Association
Green Castle
Goudhurst
Kent
Tel: Goudhurst 477

National Canine Defence League
10 Seymour Street
London W1H 5WB
Tel: 01-935 5511

They have branches scattered around, but no further north than Shropshire at present.

The Royal College of Veterinary Surgeons
32 Belgrave Square
London SW1 8QP
Tel: 01-235 4971

All vets must be registered with them in order to practise anywhere in Britain. You may telephone for any information about a vet or lodge a complaint. On July 31st of each year, the College publish a register of vets' names and addresses—very useful if you're travelling around with your pet.

The Royal Society for the Prevention of Cruelty to Animals
The Manor House
The Causeway
Horsham
Sussex RH2 1HG
Tel: Horsham 64181

Write to them for booklets, leaflets, pamphlets on all aspects of the RSPCA's work, including leaflets on the care of your dog. Published and supplied at cost price.

The People's Dispensary for Sick Animals
PDSA House
South Street
Dorking, Surrey
Tel: Dorking 81691 (code from London 0306)

With animal treatment centres, dispensaries, mobile units, and homes for strays in England, Scotland and Wales.

The Blue Cross (incorporating Our Dumb Friends' League)
Animals Hospital
Hugh Street
Victoria
London SW1
Tel: 01-834 4224/5556

Animal treatment and care centres strictly for people who cannot afford to pay.

The Blue Cross Centre
Bridge Road
Willesden
London NW10
Tel: 01-459 1796

Deals with the boarding of pets of OAPs going on holiday or into hospital.

And two books

The Dog's Guide to London by Sandy Molloy
Published by Garnstone Press

Although the information (pet shops, vets, obedience schools etc) is concentrated on the Greater London area, there's lots in this booklet to interest all dog lovers.

Pet's Welcome
W. H. Smith booklet

Contains names and addresses of 'pet-welcoming' hotels and guest houses all over Britain—invaluable when taking a pet on holiday with you.

Services

Police Stations stock illustrated leaflets with practical advice on how to protect your home. They're free—drop round and ask for them.

The Post Office
Offers many and often ignored helpful services. For details, get a copy of *The Post Office Guide* from your nearest post office or from HM Stationery Office (address of your nearest one in phone book).

British Rail
Write to:
The British Railways Board
222 Marylebone Road
London NW1 6JJ
Tel: 01-262 3232

For leaflets on their activities and often unexpected services. Or pick them up from any station.

The Design Centre
28 Haymarket
London SW1Y 4SU
Tel: 01-839 8000

and

The Scottish Design Centre
72 St Vincent Street
Glasgow G2 5TN
Tel: 041-221 6121

If you can't get along to one of the Centres personally, it's well worth dropping them a note if you're making long-term purchases for your home. Most products which pass the tests of their selection committees are given the Design Centre Award and the qualities they look for include: safe to use; well-made and durable; pleasant to handle, use and maintain; agreeable to look at; and good value for money. If you've a product identifiable only by a trade mark, and are anxious to trace the manufacturers, they'll usually come up trumps with the address! Incidentally, if you've bought something with their Award stamp on it and it doesn't come up to your expectation, they'll certainly look into your complaint.

The Association of British Launderers & Cleaners Ltd
Lancaster Gate House
319 Pinner Road
Harrow
Middx HA1 4HX

Not every laundry and dry cleaner belongs to this Association, though the majority do. If they don't, you may have no redress should something go wrong with the work.

The Motor Agents' Association Ltd
201 Great Portland Street
London W1N 6AB
Tel: 01-580 9122

The MAA sign when displayed at a garage means that this has a comprehensive method of consumer protection for the motorist, and that the Association will always be willing to investigate any complaint against it.

The Automobile Association
Fanum House
Basingstoke
Hants RG21 1BN

Like the Motor Agents' Association, the AA will investigate any claim you may have against a garage displaying the AA sign. They offer lots of useful services, from inspecting a second-hand car you want to buy to an overseas travel service (their maps and guides are excellent). They also offer a legal service and are willing to listen and help on any grouse you may have, from inadequate street lighting, unsatisfactory roads, to badly sited signs.

The Royal Automobile Club
83/85 Pall Mall
London SW1Y 5HW
Tel: 01-930 4343

Offers comprehensive weather condition service for members round the clock, and a foreign touring department and an insurance department can arrange all forms of motor insurance. Their Legal Department is always fighting the case of restrictions on the motorist. For further details, write.

The League of Safe Drivers

Apex House
Grand Arcade
Tally Ho! Corner
London N12 0EH
Tel: 01-445 1000

The Institute of Advanced Motorists

Empire House
Chiswick High Road
London W4 5TJ
Tel: 01-994 4403

Any method of becoming a better driver is worth investigating so as to do one's bit to increase safety on the roads. Write to both League and Institute for further details.

They have complementary ideas and systems you'll enjoy if you like driving.

The British Insurance Association

PO Box 538
Aldermary House
Queen Street
London EC4P 4JD
Tel: 01-248 4477

This is the central body representing over 280 British and Commonwealth insurance companies. They provide an information service for the general public and will advise which insurance company would best suit individual needs, and publish a selection of useful booklets, leaflets and films on the subject of insurance. All available free on request.

Radio & Television Retailers' Association (RTRA) Ltd

100 St Martins Lane
London WC2N 4BD
Tel: 01-836 1463/4/5/6

This Association runs a Customer Advisory Panel which investigates complaints made by members of the public. But prevention being better than cure, make sure the shop you buy your audio or other electrical equipment from has a reputable service department for any after sales needs.

The Central Bureau for Educational Visits and Exchanges

43 Dorset Street
London W1

The place to contact if you want to swop paying-guests, or just house-guests, to and fro across the Channel.

The Vegetarian Society

53 Marloes Road
London W8 6LD
Tel: 01-937 1714

They are only too pleased to help if you want to be a vegetarian. They'll supply leaflets, sample recipes, a list of restaurants, but please don't forget that stamped addressed envelope!

The Direct Sales and Service Association

47 Windsor Road
Slough, Buckinghamshire
Tel: Slough 31020

Direct selling is a boon to the housebound shopper, but it's not wise to buy from direct sales firms that aren't members of this Association. Write to them for their catalogue. Incidentally if you'd like to be a Direct Sales Representative they'll supply an address list of firms you should contact.

The British Homeopathic Association

Basildon Court
27a Devonshire Street
London W1N 1RJ
Tel: 01-935 2163

This Association is a registered charity, supported entirely by people who believe in the homeopathic system of medicine. For full details write to The Secretary (with SAE). There are homeopathic hospitals in the National Health Service both in England and Scotland.

Holidays

The Association of British Travel Agents (ABTA)
53/54 Newman Street
London W1P 4AH
Tel: 01-580 8281

Book only through travel agents belonging to this Association.

Farm Holiday Guides Ltd
18 High Street
Paisley PA1 2BX
Tel: Paisley 8455

Run, written and revised regularly by David Murdoch (travel expert) who also lists lots of other useful holiday information including furnished holidays, caravan and camping guides.

Visiting London

The London Tourist Board
4 Grosvenor Gardens
London SW1
Tel: 01-730 0791

For advice on hotels, sightseeing tours and special events. During the tourist season they also run an accommodation advice bureau on Victoria Station and at Victoria Air Terminal.

Useful books

Help yourself to London
by Michael Balfour, publisher Garnstone Press Ltd

London Streetfinder
London Guide
Visitors London
Students' London
London Walks
Alternative London
All published by Robert Nicholson

These handy-to-carry little books are crammed full of useful ideas and services London has to offer. Write to the publisher if you can't see them at your bookstall.

Kids' Guide to London
by Elizabeth Holt and Molly Perham,
published by Abelard-Schuman.

What to read
For information

Here are just a few of the many books available which can help you tackle any problem – from divorce to health and beauty.

For you and your family
Published free by the British Medical Association, they cover in simple language many subjects for the medically curious, from getting married to slimming. Write with SAE for long list of titles to:

Family Doctor Booklets
Family Doctor House
47–51 Chalton Street
London NW1

An up to date slant on child bearing in a lucid and informative book:
The Safety of the Unborn Child by Geoffrey Chamberlain (Penguin).

Divorce and After by Gerald Sanctuary (Gollancz).

Margaret Puxon's book *Family Law* (Penguin) explains in simple language the bewildering legalities when it comes to child custody.

The Camden Handbook for Parents with a Handicapped Child. This booklet, produced by the London Borough of Camden, is full of information which can make life easier for parents of a physically or mentally handicapped child. Write for details to:

Camden Public Relations Office
Town Hall
Euston Road
London NW1 5RU

Retirement

Arrangements for Old Age. This book issued by the Consumers' Association deals with problems like annuities and pensions and where to go for special services, i.e. hearing aids. It is usually stocked by your local library but if you can't find a copy write to:

The Consumers' Association
14 Buckingham Street
London WC2

Pre-Retirement and Retirement (updated 1973) by J. P. McErlean, published by author, 24 Graeme Road, Enfield EN1 3UX.

Enjoy Your Retirement by Tom Griffiths, published by David and Charles.

Dyslexia

Two useful books on dyslexia are:

The Assessment and Teaching of Dyslexic Children, a report organised by the Word Blind Centre of the Invalid Children's Aid Association (126 Buckingham Palace Road, London SW1).

Dyslexia, a guide for teachers and parents to be obtained from:

Mrs Margaret Newton
Applied Psychology Department
The University of Aston in Birmingham
College House
Gosta Green
Birmingham 4

Getting married
The Family Doctor booklet
Getting Married available free from:

Family Doctor Publications
Chalton Street
London NW1

and

The Wedding Book
published and up-dated annually by:
Newborne Publications Ltd.

Apart from tips on etiquette, bride's lists, legal details on house buying, this invaluable booklet is packed full of the latest home-making furnishings and equipment. It is often given free by jewellers if requested when buying an engagement ring!

Moving abroad
Moving House Into Europe
published for Pickfords Removals Ltd and obtainable from:

Woodhead-Faulkner Ltd
7 Rose Crescent
Cambridge CB2 3LL

If you want to live abroad this booklet will give you really practical advice on how to start the customs and laws across the Channel.

Consumer advice
Which published by:
The Consumers' Association
14 Buckingham Street
London WC2
Tel: 01-839 1222

Which is a monthly magazine compiled by a team of researchers who investigate the pros and cons of most of our everyday products. Time and again *Which* has proved that the most expensive products aren't always the most effective. They also produce more 'specialist' supplements such as *Motoring Which, Money Which, Handyman Which* etc. Details and back numbers are available.

Thomson Yellow Pages Limited
Fleet House
Farnborough
Hants
Tel: Farnborough 44391

When in doubt about who can do what—never forget the YELLOW PAGES classified directory.

How to complain

Know Your Rights by Dr Michael Winstanley and Ruth Dunkley, published by Independent Television Books.

How to Complain ... and how to avoid having to published by:
Consumer Standards Advisory Committee
British Standards Institution
2 Park Street
London W1A 2BS

How to Complain by Christopher Ward, published by Martin Secker & Warburg Ltd

Health and beauty

Recommended exercise books:
Yoga for Health by Richard Hittelman, Hamlyn, and other books by the same author (in conjunction with Yoga lessons).

Beginner's Guide to Yoga by Nancy Phelan and other books by her and co-author Michael Volin, Pelham Books.

Isometrics and you by James Hewitt, published by Universal Tandem Publishing Co.
Available at most bookshops, this book will give you lots of ideas that you can put into practice during your everyday rounds.

Herbal and natural health and beauty products
Potter's New Cyclopaedia of Botanical Herbs and Preparations by R. W. Wren, published by Health Science Press.

New Beauty by Charles Perry, Friars Press Ltd, Leicester.

Secrets of Natural Beauty by Virginia Castleton Thomas, published by Harrap.

Folk Medicine by D. C. Jarvis M.D., published by Pan Books.

Here's Health, monthly magazine, published by Newman Turner.

Culpeper Ltd. 21 Bruton Street, London, W1X 8DS (01-629 4559)
59 Ebury Street, London, SW1 (01-730 0361)
can supply detailed information and books on herbal blends of all kinds and their curative, edible and cosmetic properties.

Two good vegetarian cookbooks

Eating your way to health edited by Claire Jowenfeld, published by Faber and Faber.
Super meals without meat, published by Marshall Cavendish.

Plant care

Any by Julia Clements are both fascinating and practical.

Be Your Own House Plant Expert by Dr D. G. Hessayon (published by Pan Britannica Industries Ltd) is revised, enlarged and lucidly helpful. And if you believe that plants have feelings *The Secret Life of Plants* by Peter Tompkins and Christopher Bird (published by Allen Lane) will confirm it with amazing examples.

House Plants made Easy by Jean Taylor, published by Independent Television Books.

Actors and authors

Contacts, published by The Spotlight.

Published twice a year with essential information for anyone (animals included) with show business or literary aspirations. Names of agents, ballet and opera companies, literary agents, training schools, photographers and so much more besides.

The Writers and Artists Year Book, published by Adam and Charles Black.

For you if you want to be a freelance author or artist. It tells you, among many other things, how to set out your work to present it to editors. Hints on which publishing house or publication to choose. If you don't want to buy this book it will be in the reference section of your public library.

For your own ideas

For your own ideas

For your own ideas

For your own ideas

For your own ideas

For your own ideas

For your own ideas

ALSO AVAILABLE IN THIS SERIES

BEATING THE COST OF COOKING
Mary Berry

Beating the cost of cooking means more than economical shopping. It means making the most of your time and money. Mary Berry presents over a hundred easy, delicious and unusual receipes which will not only save you both time and money but will win your family's praise.
Mary Berry is the cookery expert of Thames Television's *Good Afternoon!* programme and cookery consultant to *Home and Freezer Digest*. She writes for *tvlife* and is the author of a number of best-selling cook books.

CARAVANNING
Barry Williams

One in every seven households in Britain enjoys a caravan holiday at some time during the year and the numbers are growing. If you are thinking of a caravan holiday, or of buying a caravan, this book is essential reading, for in it Barry Williams shows you how to choose a caravan for you and your family. He describes the different kinds of caravans available, the range of accessories and the requirements of the law. He also gives excellent ideas on how you and your family can get the most out of a caravanning holiday.
Illustrated throughout, *Caravanning* is an excellent guide for the beginner.
Barry Williams is Editor of *Camping* magazine and an enthusiastic caravanner.

HOUSE PLANTS MADE EASY
Jean Taylor

This is the practical book for the owner of one or more house plants. Illustrated throughout, the book explains the basic essentials of plant care in clear and concise detail.
The general care of plants is explained – watering, feeding, repotting and propagation – and hints are given on how to make the most attractive use of your plants.
In the second part, 64 photographs of the most popular plants are accompanied by full details of how to care for them.
Jean Taylor is an international demonstrator, teacher and judge and an enthusiastic indoor gardener. She is also well known for her two series on house plants and flower arrangement for Thames Television.

KNOW YOUR RIGHTS
Dr Michael Winstanley & Ruth Dunkley

This book is a simple guide to your rights in common situations – when buying a house, seeking welfare benefits, or taking legal action, for example.
But getting your rights inolves more than knowing what they are. The authors have therefore included lists of sources of further information – people to see and leaflets to read – to help you with your particular rights problem.
Michael Winstanley – general practitioner, journalist, author and broadcaster – currently presents a citizen's rights programme for Granada Television.
Ruth Dunkley is a social worker with wide experience of interpreting the social services to those in need and to the general public.

POWER TOOLS AT HOME
Harold King

Illustrated with nearly 200 pictures and diagrams, this is a book for everyone with modern power tools, attachments and accessories. You can easily tackle many of the jobs in the upkeep of your home and lighten the chores of gardening. You can become an expert woodworker will skill and precision

which would otherwise take years to acquire. Harold King is an expert in the Do-It-Yourself field and is the author of a number of books as well as having edited several home improvement magazines.

KNOW YOUR CAR
John Dyson

When the costs of running a car are mounting continuously you need to know how to use your car to its best advantage. Using many illustrations John Dyson in *Know Your Car* explains clearly and concisely how your car works, what can go wrong and what repairs you can easily and safely do yourself.
He also suggests sensible economic driving tips and ways to improve the safety of your car.
John Dyson is a full time author and freelance journalist (has worked on *Drive*, the AA magazine) and has been influential in bringing the problems of car safety to the public's attention.